A PASSPORT SECRETLY GREEN

by Noel Perrin

A
PASSPORT
SECRETLY
GREEN

ST MARTIN'S PRESS NEW YORK

Some of the pieces in *A Passport Secretly Green* first appeared in periodicals in the United States and Great Britain. "The Fat of the Land" was published in *New Statesman; Punch* published "A Passport Secretly Green" and "The Year of the Dog"; "All Americans Ski", "Mistah Pericles, He Dead", "The Unwilling Ear" and "The Title Game" appeared in *Vogue; The New Yorker* published "The Nightingale Song", "Don't Give Me One Dozen Roses, Give Me A Nosegay", "Golden-Voiced on the Lobby Floor", "Wake Me Up for the Hoedown" and "The Henry James Papers". The author wishes to thank the editors of those magazines for permission to reprint the pieces here.

CONTENTS

The essays here collected were written at various times during the past six years, mostly for magazines, a few especially for this book. I have not put dates on them, because I think it would look silly. On the other hand, neither have I tried to make them all seem like products of the last three months. One of them, for example, still speaks of Mr. Eisenhower as if he were our new president.

Some of the essays were written and a few were published in England. There is not much difference (in my experience) between writing for English and American magazines, but the little that is special to an English point of view I have preserved. In one or two cases the meaning of the essay depends on it.

Finally, the perceptive reader will notice that I have lived in several different places in the United States and that I tend to write of each under the guise of a native. This is not wholly a pose. There are at least three states of which I feel like a native. That's not counting Vermont, of which it is merely my ambition to feel like a native.

Thetford Center, Vt.
December, 1960

A PASSPORT SECRETLY GREEN

A passport secretly green

WHEN I WAS FIRST a research student at Cambridge, three years ago, I used to spend a great deal of my time avoiding other Americans. They in turn avoided me, and each other. If we saw another American coming, we would instantly flatten into a doorway or scurry into the nearest bookshop, holding our college scarves around our faces to distract attention.

This unsocial behavior baffled other foreign students, who generally liked to keep up home ties. Most Indians at Cambridge, for example, belonged to an elegant Asiatic club called the Majlis; they had Nehru up to speak every now and then (I met him that way) and used to give rice-and-curry dinners in each others' rooms.

East Africans of every race and color spent their

spare time in a place known as the Tusker Club, reminiscing about elephant hunts and the cheapness of Rhodesian cigarettes. Australians hung out at the Australia Club, where they were rumored to keep a wallaby; Canadians at the Canada Club. Even some of the Welsh students maintained a mysterious Celtic organization called Cymdeithas y Mabinogion.

But the eighty or so American students at Cambridge not only had no club, we wouldn't so much as exchange a baseball score. Instead we talked, not to each other, about rowing.

What was worse, none of us ever spoke a civil word to any of the blue-uniformed U.S. airmen from Lakenheath Air Base who filled the Cambridge pubs on weekends and dated the local girls. Few of us ever fraternized with the free-spending American tourists who trooped through our colleges in the spring. Purists among us were even careful to avoid Oxford, because of all the Rhodes scholars. We were frightfully keen, if I may use the sort of phrase we did, to avoid the taint of New Worldism.

I was as keen as any; and during the Easter Term of 1955 I was generally admitted to be the most inconspicuous American in residence. I went on rare occasions to Oxford, it's true, but only to visit an almost flagrantly English friend at Oriel. My police book (all foreigners living in England have police books: it's required under the Aliens Order, 1953), which I should have carried with me on such trips, I kept under a pile of socks in my bottom bureau drawer, next to my green-and-gilt passport with the signature of John Foster Dulles.

Even the three men with whom I shared lodgings served me as a sort of protective coloration. Roger Azouli, the one I knew best, was an Anglo-Egyptian of vaguely royal descent; he'd been to school most of his life in Surrey, and admired the earlier novels of Proust. He also admired a good Cambridge accent, and had one.

Marie-Claude Beauchelet, the only son of a well-to-do family from Nîmes, came next. In theory a student of international law, Marie-Claude's actual interest lay in social psychology. He spent his time at Cambridge writing a book on that of girls of the English upper middle class. "Oh, To Be a Horse," he planned to call it. Finally came our one true-born Briton, an archeologist from Staffordshire named T. F. R. Simmons.

In the company of these three I was beautifully anonymous. With Roger I often used to spend a June afternoon lounging on the meadowy Backs near King's College Chapel, while he read *Swann's Way* aloud. Sometimes, if we were wearing our college blazers, we would hear a series of clicks and look up to see a party of tourists eagerly photographing us. Once a Presbyterian minister from Detroit, Michigan, asked me to take a picture of *him* against the chapel.

"Over for long?" I asked him, sighting through his Leica.

"Just a month, I'm afraid. Oh, it must be *wonderful* to live in a place like this," he said enviously, staring at a fifteenth-century wall hung with roses.

I nodded in a proprietary, English way. "Pity you weren't here for the tulips," I said.

Equally successful was a holiday I spent once in Somerset with Marie-Claude. While he pursued psychological research with two well-bred girls from Bristol, I looked at architecture in Bath. One morning, attired as usual in my blazer and college tie, I rode my bike over to Bath Abbey to look at the angels climbing down the ladders on the façade. One look led to another, and presently I found myself inside, short guide to the Abbey in hand, peering up at the fan vaulting of the choir. As I stood there, three ladies from some southern area of the United States came up.

"I beg your pardon," said the boldest of them. "Could you tell us what sort of ceilin' that is?"

I could, and I did. Unobtrusively slipping the guidebook in my pocket, I took them all through the Abbey, giving special attention to the carving in Prior Bird's chantry. I talked about the stone quatrefoils as easily as if I had chipped out a yard or two of them myself. "This has been just delightful," sighed the leader when I had finished. "I love talkin' to you cultured Englishmen. Why, we couldn't even get our husbands to come *in* the Abbey."

My life was full of incidents like this. Once, when I was in Edinburgh just before Christmas, I even persuaded the proprietress of a small and extremely Scottish hotel to give me bed and breakfast at a shilling off her usual rate, on account of my quite genuine poverty. Her expression, when I signed the guest book and she realized that I was from New York rather than Sheffield, remains a memory beyond treasure.

There came a darker incident, though. It was all Roger's fault. I belonged in those days—I needed the money—to an organization called The Military District for Great Britain, United States Army. Its members were all American reserve officers living in England. We met twice a month at the embassy in London and did two weeks' training in the summer. The uniform needful for this training I kept well to the back of my closet in Cambridge.

Roger, who was descended, as he often told us, from the commander in chief of the Turkish army that conquered Egypt in 1517, was obsessed by this uniform. He was convinced that if he put it on he could pass for an American officer. He even had a bet with Simmons about it. Eventually, of course, he *did* put it on, and sallied forth in search of U.S. airmen. The rest of us tagged along to watch.

But there were no airmen to be found. As I later learned, Lakenheath had some kind of alert that weekend, and all passes were canceled. By nine o'clock Saturday evening we had wound up in a pub known locally as Little America, empty except for ourselves and about a dozen bewildered girls. "It's the first time in fifteen years anyone has walked through Cambridge without stumbling over half your damned Air Force," Roger was saying to me bitterly, when the door opened and three rather bleary-eyed British soldiers filed in. Roger began to quiver at once.

"Terence," he said to Simmons, tugging my Ike jacket down to his narrow hips, "the moment has come. Leftenant Roger Azouli, U.S. Army, is moving into action."

"Against the British?" Simmons asked. "Not on my ten bob. You could put on a kepi and say you were General De Gaulle, and the average English soldier would believe you. Either you find an American or the bet is off."

Roger wasn't even listening. He rose and went over to the soldiers' table, pulling out a cigarette as he went. I followed apprehensively. As we arrived, all three got to their feet.

"I say," Roger began in a clear voice, "could one of you let me have a match?" The senior of the three, a lance-corporal with a red face, reached in his pocket and took out a box of large wooden matches.

"Right you are, sir," he said, and handed them to Roger, who lit his cigarette and handed them back.

"Thanks, my man," said Roger. Then there was a silence. Roger took two puffs on his cigarette, and the soldiers looked at their feet. Roger took a deep draw.

"You chaps from around here?" he asked finally.

"Urh," said the corporal, swaying slightly. He looked as if he wanted to sit down.

"Home for the weekend, are you?" Roger persisted. "It's a beautiful town to be from."

"Urh," the corporal said again.

"I'm from the United States, myself," Roger volunteered. "A place called Philadelphia, to be exact."

"No, yer ain't," said one of the other soldiers with surprising pugnacity. "Yer ain't no American. Yer talks like an Englishman, and yer looks like a bleeding Wog."

Roger flushed at this description. For a second it

appeared that he was going to fight like a sixteenth-century Azouli.

"Come on, Roger," I said nervously. "There's no point in arguing with him. Let's get out of here."

I should never have opened my mouth. The soldier turned his full attention to me. "*Yer* a Yank," he said accusingly. "Where's your ruddy uniform? Lost it?"

"Come on, Roger," I repeated. "We ought to go."

"Is that your uniform on the Wog?" the soldier demanded. "What's the matter? Ashamed of it, are yer?"

I pulled Roger away more or less by force. Picking up Terence and Marie-Claude as we passed, we beat a shameful retreat to our lodgings.

Monday, two weeks later, which was the Fourth of July, I took some pains to wear a small, enameled American flag—it cost me one and threepence in London—prominently in my buttonhole. Roger talked of wearing one, too, but I wouldn't let him.

The nightingale song

IN MADINGLEY WOOD, near Cambridge, England, there is a grove famous for nightingales. Nettles grow thick under the trees there, and the nettles attract the nightingales—just why, nobody is quite sure, though last year my supervisor at Cambridge, where I was then doing graduate work in English, said it was because the nightingales want to sting themselves. In the Middle Ages, he pointed out, nightingales were constantly impaling themselves on thorns; they believed that the pain made them sing better. Modern nightingales, too degenerate for the thorn technique, try to encourage their melody with nettles.

One night last May, a careful observer might have seen me in the Wood, standing under a large copperbeech tree, near a patch of nettles. I was waiting to hear the nightingales sing, and I was standing because an English wood is nearly always too wet to sit down in. It wasn't just some idle love of birds that had drawn me there, either. It was my duty as an American citizen. I had just written a paper on the poetry of T. S. Eliot, and, among other things, I'd remarked that, for a modern poet, Eliot shows rare accuracy in his descriptions of nature.

"Bosh!" my supervisor had said when he returned the paper to me. "What about Eliot's nightingales? ' "Jug Jug" to dirty ears,' he quotes them in 'The Waste Land.' 'Jug Jug' to tin ears, perhaps. No nightingale ever made the noise 'Jug Jug' in his life, and so much for Mr. Eliot's rare accuracy. He'd better leave English birds to English poets."

My pride of country was aroused. As soon as I left the supervisor's rooms, I rushed to my college library and took down an enormous *Dictionary of Birds*. It was no help at all. "The song of the European or English nightingale (*Luscinia megarhyncha*) is indescribable," wrote the author evasively. Well, at least Eliot had done better than *that*. But to uphold the honor of American poetry, so must I. I decided to go and actually hear the bird for myself.

By eight o'clock that same evening, I had walked the four miles out to Madingley and was standing under my tree, listening hard. By eight-thirty, I had heard nothing but a lovesick crow. There was no use hoping for nightingales while he was around, so I sat down (getting my pants wet instantly) and returned to the literary approach. What *English* poets, I asked myself, had committed themselves on the voice of the nightingale?

Shakespeare was the obvious one to start with, but I could come up with nothing better than Bottom's boast "I will roar you as 'twere any nightingale." Bottom's ears were obviously the wrong sort for hearing nightingales, so I passed on to Shelley. Once I'd realized that the skylark was the only bird he ever wrote an ode to, I tried Keats. Of course! In "Ode to a Nightingale," Keats must have given the bird the best description it has ever had. What does Keats say? Well, as far as I could remember, Keats says that nightingales sing of summer in full-throated ease and that the time to hear them is at midnight.

It seemed a long while to wait.

When I got back to Cambridge, at about two o'clock, I was soaking wet from the hard rain that had started at twelve-thirty. My hands ached from nettle stings, and my shoes were full of mud. I was through relying on Keats for bird lore; midnight had passed without a sound. And I had made no progress toward the vindication of American poetry.

In the morning, my roommate asked me what on earth I'd done to my hands, and I told him the whole story. "Oh, well, it wouldn't have mattered if you had heard a nightingale," he said cheerfully. "Still be your word against the supervisor's, wouldn't it? Besides, the old boy is right. Nightingales don't go 'Jug Jug,' they go 'tsoo tsoo.' See Edward Thomas on this."

So I saw Edward Thomas. I went back to my college library and looked up his collected poems. "Tsoo," his nightingales cry. The sub-librarian heard me cursing softly and came over to me. I told *him* the whole story. "But Mr. Eliot's quite right," he said. "Nightingales do have a note that sounds very much like 'Jug Jug.' Beautiful it is, sir. I think you'll find it quoted in Samuel Taylor Coleridge—'The Nightingale, A Conversation Poem,' from *Lyrical Ballads*. That should satisfy your supervisor, sir."

I carried "A Conversation Poem" with me to my next supervision, and pointed out the lines to my supervisor. He read them aloud:

"And murmurs musical and swift jug jug,
And one low piping sound more sweet than all—

Well, Perrin, true enough," he said easily. "But the 'Jug Jug' counts for no more than the preliminary cough of a Wagnerian tenor. That 'low piping sound' is the real *song* of the nightingale. It's as if Eliot had announced that he was going to describe a violin concerto and then had written, 'The violins tune up, "Squeak Squeak" to dirty ears.'"

Two days later, I went to Oxford for the weekend and attended a literary tea. After the third cup, I found myself telling the whole story to my host, a sympathetic don of Lincoln College. He rubbed his hands with pleasure. "What curious nightingales you have at Cambridge," he said. "All that tuning up. Your birds must suffer from sore throats, like your lecturers. A healthy, normal nightingale—the one that lives in my garden, for example—doesn't need to warm up. He just opens his beak and starts singing. And 'Jug Jug' is an integral part of what he sings. If I were you," he concluded, pouring me a fourth cup of tea, "I should look at John Lyly's 'The Songs of Birds,' from *Campaspe,* the edition of 1584. Then I'd have a word with my supervisor."

I couldn't wait until I got back to Cambridge to speak to my supervisor. That same night, I posted him a card from Oxford. It read:

> Jug, Jug, Jug, Jug, tereu shee cryes,
> And still her woes at Midnight rise.
> —J. Lyly

When I returned to Cambridge on Monday, there was a note waiting for me.

Dear Perrin [my supervisor had written]: I didn't realize you were so serious about nightingales. I fear you are leaning on a feeble reed in John Lyly, however. His bird cries are pure literary artifice, and not even original.

Look up the Latin version of the Greek myth of Philomela, who was turned into a nightingale, and of King Tereus, who was responsible. Then tell me if you still believe in Lyly's "tereu"s—or in his "Jug, Jug"s.

Underneath, he had inscribed the following:

> Every thing did banish moan
> Save the nightingale alone.
> She, poor bird, as all forlorn,
> Leaned her breast up-till a thorn,
> And there sung the dolefull'st ditty,
> That to hear it was great pity.
> *Fie, fie, fie,* now would she cry,
> *Teru, teru,* by and by,

That to hear her so complain
Scarce I could from tears refrain.
—Richard Barnfield (1574–1627)

I was still smarting from this blow when a fresh note came on Tuesday.

Dear Perrin [it began]: I've been doing a little research on literary references to the nightingale, myself. There weren't many major poets rash enough to try to reproduce his characteristic song. But there was one: Lord Tennyson.

Unlike your Mr. Eliot, Tennyson *does* have an extraordinarily accurate ear. I quote from a minor poem of his called "The Grandmother":

The moon like a rick on fire was rising over the dale.
And whit, whit, whit, in the bush beside me chirrupt the
     nightingale.

The next morning, I presented myself at the Cambridge University Library precisely at nine-thirty, opening time. About eleven, I emerged from its bowels, grimy to the elbows from handling old books, and bearing a sheet of paper. On it were written these words from a poem titled "To Mistress Isabel Pennell," by the reasonably major poet John Skelton:

> To hear this nightingale
> Among the birdes smale
> Warbeling in the vale,
>   Dug, dug,
>   Jug, jug,
>   Good year and good luck,

With chuck, chuck, chuck,
chuck.

In the entrance hall, I ran into my supervisor. He, too, was grimy and had a slip of paper. Silently we exchanged. "Walther von der Vogelweide," his said. "Early German minnesinger. From 'Unter den Linden':

Near the woods, down in the vale,
Tandaradi!
Sweetly sang the nightingale."

My supervisor spoke first. "Perrin, suppose you meet me at Madingley pub at eight," he said. "It's going to be a long evening. We might as well start with a pint of beer."

Golden-voiced on the lobby floor

THE LATE Rabbi Max Schloessinger of New York was not a man to mince words. He particularly did not mince them when he came to speak of cantors, a melodious group who occupy in twentieth-century Judaism somewhat the same position that ministers of music do in the Presbyterian Church, except that where a minister of music usually just directs a choir of other people's voices, a cantor is expected to be his own first tenor as well.

It was Dr. Schloessinger's profound love of Jewish liturgy that made him suspicious of cantors. Cantors, he felt, were anti-liturgical. (Rabbis, of course, in common with priests, Church of England clergymen, imams and mullahs, are pro-liturgical.) As he liked to point out, cantors once in the past got control of the Jewish service of worship, and when they did they made it into a kind of singing contest or Sabbath opera, to the confounding of rabbis, true religion, and good taste. He was convinced that given half a chance they would do so again.

The trouble began, Dr. Schloessinger has written, about fourteen hundred years ago, with the invention of a kind of hymn known as a *piyyut*. (The name derives from a Greek word which means simply "poetry.") The earliest *piyyut* writers, or *payyetan*, were French and Spanish rabbis, who, naturally, handled the new form with decorum; but by A.D. 750 or so cantors had moved in and taken over. Half the cantors in Europe were busy composing *piyyutim*, and what is worse, lustily chanting their products in synagogue. A decline in religious standards followed at once.

For one thing, Dr. Schloessinger complained, the cantors in their frantic race to compose the most *piyyutim* began stealing tunes from pagans. French folk song or Moorish chant, it made no difference; the cantors snatched them. These were "foreign melodies taken from non-Jewish sources," Dr. Schloessinger wrote darkly, and they had no place in the synagogue.

It was no better, however, when the cantors used proper Hebrew melodies for their hymns. Musical notation in the eighth century was fairly primitive, and the corpus of traditional Jewish music hardly existed in written form. It depended for its sanctity, rather, on an oral tradition going back two thousand years and carefully guarded during all that time by a series of devoted rabbinical scholars. But the cantors, of course, were artists not scholars, and they were much more interested in devising something good for next Friday's service than they were in preserving tradition. The result was that through the years they revised the old tunes "consciously or unconsciously, in accordance with their individual tastes, which were often very poor."

Why did the medieval rabbis put up with this kind of outrage? The answer is that they didn't. They were as firm as Dr. Schloessinger himself in condemning the new music, but no one would listen to them. "It is true," says Dr. Schloessinger, "that in the ninth century *hazzanim* [as cantors were then called] skilled in *piyyutim* were rejected, but the rejection was only temporary." For in one brief century the cantors and their gaudy hymns had obtained "both over the ritual and over the congregation, an almost limitless influence."

Worse was to come. Inflamed by their success with the *piyyutim,* the medieval cantors began to insert more and more chanting of all sorts into the Sabbath service. It became customary to chant whole sections of the Sedarim or sacred readings. The rabbi, who had formerly recited the lesson in a dignified speaking voice, could sit and listen. And in time even chanting ceased to satisfy the triumphant cantors. "Their vanity," wrote Dr. Schloessinger, "also led them to unsuitably prolong single notes and to introduce interludes of song." They composed solos called *sebarot,* "which they prolonged at will," apparently taking frequent encores and repeating the best parts

polyphonically. The rabbis might stir and dart meaningful glances, but the cantors went right on singing
their *sebarot*. They went on for centuries.

By Shakespeare's time, the more extreme exhibi-
tionists among them had even got into the habit of
putting their hands on their throats and vibrating
their fingers up and down, "evidently to facilitate
trilling or the producing of high notes." The only result of *this* sort of thing, Dr. Schloessinger said coldly,
was to make the services run overtime, which "naturally caused general weariness, and hence there re-
sulted a great deal of disorder." And he quoted with
approval the dictum of a sixteenth-century rabbi who
said that a cantor in synagogue "should not look about
him nor move his hands restlessly"—much less strum
them on his throat—and, in fact, granting him to have
"an agreeable voice," should devote most of his effort
to staying humble and blameless in character.

This is not, however, advice that cantors seem very
often to have taken. They do not seem to be taking it
now. The specific problem of the *piyyutim* was
eventually dealt with by the Reform movement of
Judaism, in the nineteenth century. Rabbi Schloessinger could write in 1925 that they were seldom sung
any more. And Rabbi Francis L. Cohen could write
the same year that "the efforts of a century of work"
by devoted rabbis seemed finally to have brought
cantors and synagogal music under some sort of control.

But with the exuberant vanity so characteristic of
all artists, the cantors have refused to stay suppressed.
If Rabbi Schloessinger could look at the cantoral

scene in 1959, he would find his darkest fears con-
firmed. Rabbis are once again moving into eclipse,
and once again cantors are asserting their almost limitless influence over ritual and over congregation.

I base this judgment chiefly on a rapt perusal I have
been making, for the past couple of springs, of Passover advertising in the travel section of the New
York *Times*. Passover is, of course, one of the three
great festivals of the Jewish year, and is intimately
allied with Easter. It has traditionally been celebrated
in small groups, very privately. Jesus, for example,
celebrated it in an upper room with just the twelve
disciples (who addressed him as "Master," or
"Rabbi"). If there was a cantor present, the Gospels
do not mention him.

The advertisements that I've been reading with
such interest mention little else but. These days it has
become popular in America to celebrate Passover in
large groups, often at resort hotels, and that means
advertising. The several hundred hotels that cater to
the Passover trade are all using cantors as lures, com-
peting avidly with each other for the best-known ones
(of whom there are a surprisingly large number), and
hardly thinking to mention rabbis at all. It's the story
of the *piyyutim* all over again: the rabbis laid the
foundation, but the cantors live in the house.

Take, for example, the very large structure in South
Fallsburg, New York, known as Schenk's Paramount
Hotel. Schenk's whetted expectation for many weeks
before Passover this year by promising that religious
services at the hotel would be conducted by "The
Incomparable Cantor Avrum Dubow." The advertise-

ments included a photograph of Mr. Dubow, and a handsome fellow he looked, with his hairline mustache and rich vestments. In smaller type, as if it were a kind of afterthought, Schenk's mentioned that its incomparable singer would be "assisted" by Rabbi Moshe Gershon.

Laurel in the Pines at Lakewood, New Jersey, was more one-sided still. Its advertisements promised the eager guest "The Renowned Cantor Leibele Waldman" to conduct services in "Our Own Synagogue," and then, eschewing so much as the dignity of first names, added casually that the kitchen would be "under supervision of Rabbis Charlop and Reichman." That's the sort of writing that would have made Dr. Schloessinger's blood boil.

It's nothing, though, to what The Breakers, in Atlantic City, put in the paper. The Breakers lured guests with a vision of Cantor Chaim Shapiro and the Henry Spector Choir of "18 Glorious Voices in Our New Synagogue on Lobby Floor." Then, lapsing into the familiar small print, the management listed the following supplementary attractions: "Gala Floor Show. Music. Dancing. Indoor Heated Swimming Pool. Steam Room. Sun Lamps. Cocktail Lounge. Hot & Cold Sea Water Baths. Sun Deck. Dietary Laws Supervision. Rabbi Moishe Shapiro." I think it's coming after the sun lamps that stings most.

Still, Moishe Shapiro fared better than the bulk of his colleagues. Six of the resorts out of nine failed to mention their rabbis by name at all. I'm not sure whether some of them even had rabbis for Passover.

Every last one had a cantor, and spoke kindly of him, too.

The advertisement of the New Irvington Hotel of Lakewood, New Jersey, to take one at random, urged patrons to come there "For an Unforgettable Passover." Unforgettable on account of whom? Who but "The Famous Cantor Isadore Hyatt"? Cantor Hyatt even *looks* famous in the large accompanying photograph.

Kutsher's Country Club, Monticello, New York, was not backward in its claims, either. "Passover-Time Is a Many-Pleasured Thing at Kutsher's," the management announced in large black type, just above a picture of Cantor Sholom Katz. A block of text to one side details some of the pleasures. Chief among them was an evening of "variety entertainment" which was to be "highlighted" by a concert starring (their word) Cantor Katz.

At the same time Brown's of Loch Sheldrake, New York, a hotel that "leaves you breathless" and that is the favorite resort of Jerry Lewis, had golden-voiced Cantor Abraham Wolkin on hand. The picture, in this case, was the picture of Jerry Lewis, but the voice was the voice of Wolkin.

Those who enjoyed Passover at the fabulous—and friendly—Raleigh Hotel in South Fallsburg, New York, fared equally well. They heard the glorious-voiced Cantor Bela Herskovits, whose life story thrilled millions on television's "This Is Your Life." The Waldemere, in Livingston Manor, New York, offered even more thrills than the Raleigh, and easily the greatest of them was the singing of "world-famous

Cantor Mordecai Yardeini accompanied by the renowned Kazimirsky choir." And at The Pines, South Fallsburg, New York, Phil and May Schweid were proud to present "America's Foremost Dramatic Cantor," who is, of course, Sidney Shicoff.

Does this list sound as if it included all the really prominent cantors? Don't be misled. A full rendering would include a number of other quite reputable songsters. For example:

At the La Reine Bradley, Bradley Beach, New Jersey: world-famous Cantor Samuel Vigoda.

At the Coronet, Miami Beach, Florida: renowned Cantor Charles B. Bloch.

At the Albion, Asbury Park, New Jersey: famous Israeli Cantor Moses Dattner.

At the St. Charles, Atlantic City, New Jersey: world-famous Cantor Jacob Fox.

At Saltz's Hotel, Mount Freedom, New Jersey: renowned Cantor Irving Rogoff.

At The Willows, Lakewood, New Jersey: "elaborate services by famed cantor," who later turned out to be Cantor Morris Doberman.

I've saved the best for last. Cantor Moshe Koussevitzky is not only every bit as much a world figure as Cantors Waldman, Hyatt, Yardeini, Vigoda, Fox, and the rest, he is a man of really staggering activity. During Passover this year, he seemed to be everywhere at once. In Atlantic City, billed as the famous Cantor of Warsaw and sponsored by a group of nine motels, he gave a thrilling liturgical and operatic concert. In another part of the city and billed simply as "World-Famous Cantor Moshe Koussevitzky," he was the regular Passover cantor for the Chelsea Hotel. Up in South Fallsburg, New York, at the Flagler Hotel, where golden-voiced Cantor Benjamin Alpert was the regular officiant, he flashed in to give a special concert as "International Tenor Star Moshe Koussevitzky."

I may read too much into this last billing. But in it I think I detect the first signs that the cantors are beginning to overreach themselves, as they did with the *piyyutim*. Artistic vanity ruined the cantors once, and it may again. What I mean is, Mr. Koussevitzky's appearance at the Flagler did not even require notice of his cantoral status. It's enough that he is an international tenor star, a golden voice soaring in the lobby. For all the guests know, he might in his private religion be a Seventh-day Adventist.

And when the standards begin to fall, there's no telling where they will stop. Already at the Miami Beach Exhibition Hall things have gone far enough so that the man engaged for the two most important nights of Passover was Jan Peerce, "renowned Metropolitan Opera tenor." It's true enough that Mr. Peerce has been a cantor in good standing, but the advertisements don't bother to mention it. But perhaps the danger is clearest at Grossinger's, of Grossinger, New York, which is probably the most famous resort of them all. At Grossinger's, *one week* before Passover this year, lording it in the lobby as "honored guests," were five New York State senators: Warren Anderson, of Binghamton; Earl Brydges, of Niagara Falls; Walter E. Cooke, of Brooklyn; John H. Farrell, of

Manhattan; and Thomas Mackell, of Queens. Not a cantor in the lot.

Where's the threat in that? "The last-mentioned gentleman," Grossinger's paid for space in the *Times* to announce, is "affectionately known as 'The Singing Senator,' because of his melodious voice."

Five years from now, who knows what renowned cantor may find himself standing in the shadows with the rabbis, listening while the melodious voice of Senator Mackell lifts in a thrilling concert of operatic and liturgical music? Which liturgy one shudders to think.

All Americans ski

I HAVE ENGLISH COUSINS. They live in Wiltshire, a mother and two adolescent daughters, and it was with them I went to Switzerland a few winters back. I didn't especially want to go to Switzerland: the question of what I wanted to do somehow never arose.

"Where are you spending Christmas?" Cousin Odette asked me in early November, when I had driven over for the weekend from Cambridge University, where I was then an overseas research student. I explained that I was thinking of going to Marseilles to eat bouillabaisse.

"What? All by yourself?" she said in horror. "No, no, we can't have that. People should spend Christmas with their families. You ought to be in New York with your mother. But since you're not, you'd better come to Switzerland with us. Get yourself a second-class railway ticket to Klosters. You can rent skis and ski boots after we arrive.

"You do ski, don't you?" she asked as an after-thought.

I had my mouth open to reply that I skied a little as a child. I was going to add that when I reached years of discretion—in my case it happened my junior year at college—I took my skis and presented them to the twelve-year-old son of our family dentist, a man I've never liked. I didn't get the chance. My cousin Jennifer answered for me. "Of course he skis, Mother," she said impatiently. "All Americans do. Peter Linton says the entire Oxford ski team, except one Canadian, is American." She almost melted me with an admiring, quite uncousinly smile.

"Can you ski-jump?" asked my cousin Susan, who was sixteen and had butter-colored hair.

"Not I," I said, speaking before I thought. All three of my cousins stiffened. "I mean, I used to as a boy in school," I hastily corrected myself, "though I've done practically none since. Still, one never quite forgets, does one?" They unstiffened.

It was snowing hard when our train pulled into Klosters some five weeks after the evening I speak of, and it continued to snow for three days. The youths of the village, a uniformly muscular group, were busy all day every day, and at night with torches, keeping open what became progressively narrower ski trails. Well before the third day they had become almost tunnels through the waist-high snow, and far too narrow for the old-fashioned plow turn I learned in Dutchess County, New York. They remained, however, ample for the chic Christies practiced by my cousins and most of the three hundred or so other tourists in the village.

"Isn't the snow beautiful!" exclaimed Odette that third morning, lacing up her ski boots. "I do wish it would stop. No, Susan," she added, frowning at her younger daughter, "you must lace them tighter. Ski boots aren't tight enough until they hurt." She gave one of her own laces a tug that nearly broke the rawhide. Then she looked up again, and I could see her eyes begin to drill into Jennifer's boots. It was obvious whose ankles would be X-rayed after that. Reluctantly I bent over to finish cutting off the circulation in both feet.

We were on our way to join Class Three of the little ski school in Klosters. Class Three is the point at which you cease clomping with painful, slanted steps up nasty little hills behind the hotel, and begin to be towed up much larger and nastier hills on ski lifts. I was by no means ready to leave Class Two, and I knew it. So did the instructor, but like the rest of us he stood profoundly in awe of Odette. Odette felt it was "better" for our little group to advance together.

I knew Odette's feelings, because the night before I had suggested to her that I do my advancing separately. It was painfully clear, I said, that she and both girls were better skiers than I. None of them needed any more practice on what the Swiss with their usual wild humor call the nursery slopes. I, to the contrary, needed a great deal.

"Nonsense," said Odette briskly. "A big, strapping fellow like you—why, in a week you'll be skiing better than any of us."

"Oh, no, really, I won't," I replied earnestly, hunching down in a semiconscious attempt to look smaller.

All three of my cousins, the tallest of whom is Jennifer at about 5′4″, cocked their heads to one side and looked up at me, like three robins examining a grackle. "You men," they chorused with what I still believe was sincere admiration. "You're so modest, so brave." The next morning, as I've noted, I went into Class Three.

About twenty minutes later I left it again. That is, I fell off the ski lift, taking with me in the upset my companion on the T-bar, a middle-aged Dutch woman of terrifying competence. My skis had crossed and then mounted over her skis, and we landed more or less in each other's arms in the neighboring deep snow. "You must keep your skis ab-so-lute-ly parallel," she told me as we separated ourselves (her English was terrifyingly competent, too), and she proceeded to give me a lesson in how to do it right there by the ski trail, first, with great rapidity, tramping out a little clear space in the four-foot snow.

We were able to rejoin the class in about three-quarters of an hour. Jennifer was very solicitous, and thought, or seemed to think, that it was the Dutch woman who had knocked me off; she explained that the Dutch, having no hills of their own, were always hopeless skiers.

This act of cousinly faith didn't keep me from crossing my skis again on the next trip up, but happily I was now riding at the very tail of the class, in company with the instructor, and I think only a few people saw me fall. Furthermore, the instructor actually did succeed during the remainder of the morning in teaching me how to keep my skis parallel, and I made three ascents on the T-bar that afternoon with aplomb and skill. In the evening I took Jennifer dancing at another and grander hotel than our own, and told her tall stories about college life in America.

That was Christmas Eve. The following day, of course, school was canceled. At breakfast I suggested innocently that we use our freedom to take the train up to Davos and go to service at the English church there. "On the first clear day we've had?" inquired Odette. "I don't know about you, but *I* intend to practice turns. I'm still fearfully rusty." We all practiced turns: they Christies, I snow plows.

School resumed promptly on the twenty-sixth, and on that day our little unit advanced to Class Four. To my horror the instructor of Four made no protest whatsoever when Odette informed him that she was promoting me. He didn't even shrug one of those resigned Continental shrugs. Probably *he* had spent the evening with the instructors of Classes Two and Three.

In Four, one is too advanced merely to be dragged up large hills in the embrace of a T-bar lift. Instead one is borne thousands of feet up precipitous mountains, swaying perilously in a kind of aerial chair. Susan, who had the chair in front of me, was ecstatic.

"Herr Klumpp says it's a straight three-mile run back down," she shouted to me.

I was a little ecstatic myself, when we first started down, though I think for different reasons. Herr Klumpp, incredibly, considering that he was Swiss and held an official position at that, had his information wrong. The topmost mile of the run did not go straight down. It was distinctly roller-coastery.

There were two almost level stretches and even a brief uphill bit. It was, in short, my kind of mountain. I rather enjoyed skiing it. I maneuvered along, not hurrying, not falling, and very much in control. Ten minutes after I started I came round a bend in good order, doing a steady six miles an hour, and ran past the mistress of a German millionaire who was staying at the larger hotel. She was sprawled in a snowdrift, squeaking.

Just beyond her the trail widened slightly, and I was able to snow-plow deftly to a stop. I reversed direction in the approved Klosters Class-One manner, inched gracefully back, and helped the girl to her feet. She squeaked her thanks, managing to look even more blue-eyed than usual. I read my superiority to middle-aged Teutonic millionaires in that look, and reacted instinctively.

Instead of resuming motion my normal way, which was to lean a few inches forward and wait, I tipped my cap to the girl, crouched, made a bold gesture with both ski poles, and shot off down the trail. The next three miles were, as Herr Klumpp had said, a straight downhill run.

It was terror, I suppose, that kept me upright. Unable to reduce my speed in any way, I saw no alternative to doing the entire run in one hideous crescendo, much as Odette, Jennifer, and Susan must have done a few minutes earlier. Eventually I passed the speed of sound, or at least I distinctly heard Doppler's effect when I hurtled past a group of loud-voiced children at the very bottom of the mountain. Then I careened sideways into an enormous mound of snow that had been cleared off an open-air skating rink, just this side of Klosters. Snow flew about twenty feet in the air. My skis made a strenuous effort to follow. But, of course, being attached to my feet, they couldn't.

When the debris had settled, I conducted a brief self-examination. I was dismayed, certainly. My head was completely bowed, yes. Bloody it was not. I unbuckled my harness where I lay, and stood up. My legs, to my considerable surprise, supported me. Brushing past the disappointed cluster of children (they seemed to want to haul me into the village on a big sled they had), I made my way to the upper end of the village street, into the hotel, and up to my room. There I ordered tea sent up and lay quietly down to meditate.

After about an hour I got up again and took a long, thoughtful bath. I put my skiing clothes back on and took a horse and sleigh to the railroad station. The ticket clerk spoke neither English nor French, but we managed in broken Italian. I bought a whole series of tickets. Then I went in search of my cousins. They had just come in.

"Where did you go?" asked Jennifer. "We haven't seen you all afternoon. Did you come in early?"

I ignored that. "Odette," I said, "I've been doing a little figuring about dates. I really must get on to France. If I'm going to reach Marseilles in time for New Year's, I ought to leave Klosters not later than Tuesday. That only leaves tomorrow, and tomorrow I've promised myself to have a look at Davos."

"You're an idiot to leave now," said Odette, frowning. "We'll be entering Class Five on Tuesday. That's where the fun begins. Why can't you spend New Year's here? I thought you were going to."

"I'm afraid I really must get on to Marseilles."

"Well, if you must, you must." She pondered a minute. "At least the girls and I will spend your last day with you. Tomorrow we can have a nice ski in the morning and take the train to Davos right after lunch."

"Oh, I particularly want to see the churches," I said quickly. "I've gotten very interested in undercrofts. There's no need to drag you three into them. I'll go up ahead in the morning and meet you at the station after lunch."

A certain startled comprehension became visible in Odette's eyes, and she let the subject drop. "Come along, girls," she said to her daughters. "Knock the snow off your skis. We've just time to wax them before the hockey match."

She started out, followed by Susan, but Jennifer lingered a second. "You must come to the match, too, and explain everything to me," she said gently. "I expect you played quite a lot in college.

Early Tuesday morning I boarded the train for Zurich; and by Thursday I was standing on the Marseilles water front watching a fisherman in a leather apron sell live eels, which he chopped into sections, depending on how much live eel the purchaser wanted. Presently I bought an entire eel, which I carried about two hundred feet away and put back into the water. Then I wandered off to see that block of flats of Le Corbusier's on the Boulevard Michelet. I have never gone back to Switzerland. I find I can't stand Swiss architecture.

Mistah Pericles, he dead

A FEW MONTHS AGO I saw one of those movies about confused intellectuals and how love unconfuses them. It was a classic of its kind. The heroine is a girl who works in a secondhand bookstore and spends her evenings studying philosophy. Then she snaps out of it and becomes a famous model. Later on she marries a fashion photographer who is even more famous than she, and gives up reading. I enjoyed every minute I was in the theater.

There was one scene, however, along toward the end of the film, that set me to wondering. The photographer has taken the girl to Paris to do an important series on her for his magazine. He is simultaneously wooing her, but with no success whatever. She still prefers secondhand books. Then one afternoon, as he is setting up his camera, the girl makes a shy announcement. Trembling a little from the unexpectedness of it all, she tells him she's just realized that she loves posing for the magazine, and she loves being in Paris, and she loves *him*. Does he respond, as one might expect, by assuring her in some fairly vibrant way of his own deep passion? No, he does not. He looks at her as if she had had a sudden relapse and started quoting Aristotle. Then he reels a couple of steps backward. "Well, whaddaya know?" he blurts in honest surprise.

At the time I explained this to myself as just one of those lines they write in Hollywood. It's extreme, I admit, but it belongs to a recognizable genre. Anyone who goes to the movies even occasionally has met similar lines. What they constitute are anticlimaxes, failures to respond, de-articulations. That they are deliberate there can be no doubt. Nor is there much question as to their function. Their function is to reassure us average moviegoers that everybody else is average, too—to satisfy us ordinary, prose-talking citizens that deep down all men talk prose, even Cyrano de Bergerac, if you could only catch him off guard. It's like Hollywood's other assumption, that no one *really* likes classical music, and if you could only get the repressed young piano student away from her domineering teacher and into a low-cut dress, she would soon abandon Bach fugues and begin thumping out some pretty erotic jazz.

In terms of my particular film, I felt that the photographer's grunt-like answer was the girl's final penance for having been an intellectual in the first place. I didn't take it seriously, any more than she herself did. (She got engaged to the man two scenes later.) Hollywood's realism, I comfortably concluded, is the most unrealistic thing in the place.

Just as I was concluding this, however, a piece of dialogue from real life flashed into mind. It was foreign real life, at that. I found myself remembering that meeting of British Commonwealth explorers at the South Pole last year, and the strikingly unoratorical way in which its participants expressed themselves. These, as we will all remember, were Sir Vivian Fuchs, the great English geographer, and Sir Edmund Hillary, the world-famous conquerer of Mount Everest. Sir Francis Drake would hardly have recognized their style.

Sir Edmund spoke first. "Hello, Bunny," he greeted Fuchs, his voice a little solemn.

Sir Vivian rose to the occasion. "Damn glad to see you, Ed," he replied, there amid the eternal snows.

It was a scene to stir the soul. Mine was stirred. I felt, as a matter of fact, as if someone had slipped a Mixmaster into it. Out of its depths began to rise, like bubbles from a swamp, the whole public utterance of our day.

Through my ears began to ring, for example, some of the characteristic phrases of President Eisenhower. Is he being well received as chief executive? "A fellow never knows," says Mr. Eisenhower. How does he feel about Russian imperialism? "Doggone it, that's not right," comments the President. Does Mr. Eisenhower approve of foreign words (like *mot* or *juste*)? "By Jiminy, our own language is rich enough, why don't we learn to use it!" he patriotically counters.

Presently my mind went echoing back to the trumpet utterance of former President Truman. I recalled vividly Mr. Truman's demurral when he was first offered the vice-presidency by President Roosevelt in 1944. "I don't want the darned thing," he demurred. I lived again his first recorded words on his first day as president in 1945. "C'mon in, Tony," they were. I recalled *his* reaction to a minor twist of Russian policy, a few months later. "Ain't that sumpin'?" he marveled.

Religious oratory surged into memory, too. I heard again the great culminating appeal of the foremost preacher of our time. I tingled as I listened to the familiar words. "So now, while the choir sings softly, 'Just as I am, without one plea,' you come down and say, 'Billy, tonight I accept Jesus Christ.'"

By now I was almost as full of excitement as the heroine of the movie on the day she fell in love with the photographer. I knew I was on the edge of a major discovery. All these accents were too much alike for it to be sheer coincidence. And finally I realized that the mid-twentieth century has brought an abrupt change in the way men talk.

It's a change for the better, I expect. What we have done is to purge our speech of rhetoric. It was time. Look at what rhetoric did to our ancestors. Our ancestors were rhetoricians almost to a man—and they went around polishing their marriage proposals in advance, practicing sermons in front of mirrors, and deliberately planting eloquence in their political addresses. They never asked themselves if this was being sincere. And of course it wasn't being. It was being staggeringly hypocritical. But today we all of us have learned to be as plain and honest as old shoes. We say what we really think. Avoiding pretense, we employ the simple, unaffected phrases that naturally occur to us. Even at the high moments of history we do.

Let me demonstrate. I'll bet if Samuel F. B. Morse, for example, were sending the first telegraph message now instead of in 1844, he would choose to word it rather differently. "What hath God wrought?" Morse dramatically asked in 1844, just as if he didn't know that he had invented the new device himself. Such mock-modesty turns the stomach. He would not, I think, be guilty of it today. "Hi, telegraph fans! This is Sam Morse, bringing you the greatest communications advance since the eardrum," he would more likely send clicking over the wires now.

Or take the case of Bishops Hugh Latimer and Nicholas Ridley, who were burnt at the stake in Oxford, England, on October 16, 1555. Episcopal dignity or no episcopal dignity, I am confident that they would play the scene in a vastly lower key now. Bishop Latimer would *not* look at Bishop Ridley as the fire was being built and intone, "Be of good comfort, Master Ridley, and play the man; we shall this day light such a candle, by God's grace, in England, as I trust shall never be put out," rightly rejecting the sentiment as contrived. I feel that instead he would say what was really on his mind. "For heaven's sake, Nick, smile," I can hear him urgently whisper. "Think of the photographers."

The language of the future, assuming there is a future, promises to be even more natural and unaffected than that used at present. I have a friend who tells me his mind boggles when he tries to imagine what kinds of remarks will be made on great public occasions five or ten or twenty years from now. Mine doesn't. I have a very clear vision of what it will all be like. It will be like this:

On the first landing of human beings on the moon, 1964:

Antique Style (landing by U.S. rocket)—"In the name of the Congress of the United States of America and of the General Assembly of the United Nations, I claim this satellite for the dominion of man."

New Style (U.S.)—"Whaddaya mean, me first? You're the leader, ain't ya?"

Antique Style (landing by Russian rocket)—"In the name of the Supreme Soviet and of the imperishable spirit of Marxism, I proclaim this the People's Satellite for Freedom."

New Style (U.S.S.R.)—"This is no time for jokes, Vladimir. It does not in the *least* resemble Outer Mongolia."

On winning the men's singles at Wimbledon, 1966:

Antique Style—"Well played, sir! That last set is the finest tennis I've seen since Budge beat Von Cramm in '37."

New Style—"Psst! Want to turn pro, buddy?"

On accepting the Nobel prize in chemistry, 1969:
Antique Style—"I come in a spirit of profound humility. The prize is being awarded, I feel, not so much to me as to chemistry itself. I especially rejoice to think that despite his being over eighty now, my first chemistry teacher, Professor Frederick Carver, is here today to see one of his old students receive the award that's the logical outcome of his kind of teaching."

New Style—"Two years ago, when I first discovered perturbium, I said to myself, Harold, my boy, if there's any justice in the world you'll get the Nobel out of this. Frankly, folks, the big attraction was the cash. I figure I'll net a clean forty thousand bucks."

After the first around-the-world jet flight to take less than an hour, 1974:
Antique Style—"I flew at 800,000 feet. You're terribly alone up there, with the black sky around you and the green earth far, far down beneath you, and the stars blazing brighter than you ever believed was possible."

New Style—"Sorry, chaps. I went so damn' fast I didn't see a thing."

On the shooting of the last herd of wild elephants in Africa, 1992:
Antique Style—"I'm not ashamed to admit it, there was a lump in my throat when I lifted my rifle and fired at that huge, gray old leader, the last wild elephant there'll ever be. They had to go, of course. With five billion people alive, there's no room for elephants. We need every square inch for crops. But it made me pretty sick to have to do it."

New Style—"Feel? They didn't feel a thing. The Land Resources Commission arranged to have an instant-acting anesthetic in every bullet. Hunh? You mean *me*? Well, I didn't feel anything, either. Whaddaya think I am, a sentimentalist?"

Lewd Lewis and how he was saved

IN THE SPRING of 1796, about a hundred and
forty years before the birth of Françoise Sagan, an
undersized English adolescent named Matthew
Lewis published his first novel. To no one's surprise,
the book was an instant and howling success. It had
everything: high-born characters, racy plot, a bit of
blasphemy, and lots of youthful cynicism. It also con-
tained an acute and detailed analysis of the psychology of sex. This analysis centered on the person of a
moody Spanish clergyman named Ambrosio.

Everyone was most deliciously shocked. Coleridge,
writing a review of the new novel in 1797, gave its
sales a good prod by complaining long and loudly of
the impiety. Byron, reading it for his own pleasure in

1813 ("I looked yesterday at the worst parts," he noted in his journal for December sixth), screamed at the sex. He found Lewis's attitude toward sex jaded and corrupt, his descriptions of passion decadent. "It is to me inconceivable how they could have been composed by a man of only twenty," he wrote indignantly in his journal. He would perhaps have been yet more indignant if he had known that Lewis actually composed much of the book when he was eighteen, and a very bored young diplomat at the British Embassy to the Hague.

Lewis's own father, a millionaire slave-owner and member of Parliament, was disturbed by the book; and so were a number of the leading men at court, including that Viscount Lewisham who a few years later as the Earl of Dartmouth was to combine in his person the three great if somewhat oddly assorted offices of Lord Chamberlain to His Majesty's Household, Master of the Revels, and President of the Society for the Suppression of Vice. By late 1797 there was even some rather loud talk, led by Beilby Porteus, Lord Bishop of London, of having the book banned.

Lewis was the sort of person to take this lying down. He took most things lying down. Few men in the history of English literature can have been as eager not to stand up for their art as he was. He even helped other people not to stand up for theirs. On one occasion in 1804, his mother—a reckless beauty who had been cast out by old Mr. Lewis and whom young Matthew supported out of his pocket money—decided that *she* would write a novel. Lewis forbade

it. It would upset his sisters, he said, especially Maria,
the elder one. Maria had recently married the heir
to a baronetcy, a well-bred and rather conventional
young man named Henry Lushington. "Her mother's
turning novel-writer would (I am convinced) not only
severely hurt [Maria's] feelings, but would raise the
greatest prejudice against her in her husband's
family," Lewis wrote his mother.

Mrs. Lewis, eyes flashing, replied that the prej-
udices of Maria's husband's relatives were no concern
of hers.

"I did not expect you to consider the feelings of the
Lushington family," Lewis answered in quiet reproof,
"but Maria's interest; which is certainly that she
should be loved and respected by her husband's relations; and from what I know of them I am persuaded that she would not be better thought of by
them for having an authoress for her mother." The
novel remained unwritten.

This was all in the future, of course. Back in 1797,
Lewis's own novel had not only been written and
published, but was outselling most books in England.
It had taken a while for the opposition to get organ-
ized. By the time Bishop Porteus was baying for suppression and Viscount Lewisham was shaking his
head in disapproval and old Mr. Lewis had begun to
repent of buying his son a seat in Parliament (he
gave it to the boy as a twenty-first birthday present),
the book had raced through two editions and was just
making a triumphal debut in Ireland.

Now if ever was the time to lie down and play
dead. Lewis did. He ordered his publisher to take the

third edition off the market and destroy it. Then he sat down and wrote his father a letter of formal apology for causing so much fuss. And then, carrying a copy of *The Monk,* he paid a call on his sister Maria.

What happened next is something of a mystery. Lewis himself afterwards claimed that in response to popular demand he himself eagerly expurgated his own book. A bowdlerized copy with the changes made in his handwriting survives in the British Museum. Some observers, however, myself included, are inclined to give the bulk of the credit to Maria, the future Lady Lushington. It is a matter of record that Lewis did submit his next manuscript to her and that she cleaned it up with zest. Or, as a friend of the family named Margaret Baron-Wilson put it, in her biography of Lewis, Maria "with the delicate tact of a correct judgement, and a pure and pious mind, struck out, with her own hand, all the passages . . . which she imagined might be construed into offenses."

Whoever was responsible, the results are remarkable indeed. Maria (if it was indeed she) did a good deal more than strike out the possibly offensive words and passages. She replaced them with other words and passages of her own choosing, words and passages which brought an entirely new spirit (a literal one, with wings) into the book. Between the suppressed third edition and the expurgated fourth, *The Monk* underwent a metamorphosis from the almost clinical account of sexual frustration familiar to modern readers into a cautionary tale, pointing the moral that sexual experience outside of marriage breeds trouble for all concerned.

If permitted to argue in her own defense, Maria could have pointed out that *The Monk* of the first three editions *needed* a new spirit. Undeniably the book is a trifle sensational. Ignoring one or two side-plots and the blood-smeared ghost of a long-dead nun, it is the story of the Abbot Ambrosio aforesaid. Don Ambrosio is the leading preacher and the most famous mortifier of the flesh in all Madrid, perhaps in all of Spain. The Man of Holiness, as the Madrilenos proudly call him, is also one of the best-looking men in southern Europe, no more than thirty, and in the full vigor of manhood.

Very early in the novel he has the misfortune to be seduced in his own cell by an extraordinarily beautiful girl who has gained access to the monastery in the guise of a novice. The rest of the book describes his steady moral decline, culminating in the inadvertent rape of his own sister. In the end he is borne off to hell by his original seductress, who is now revealed to be no girl at all, nor even human, but a literal agent of the devil, a Gothic variant of C. S. Lewis's Screwtape and Wormwood.

Thus, taken in broad outline, *The Monk* is colorful but pious. Beilby Porteus himself couldn't quarrel with the propriety of a lecherous monk's being carried off to hell. What caused the sensation, of course, and what he did quarrel with, was the detailed accuracy with which Lewis described the causes of Ambrosio's departure. It is this accumulation of almost Freudian detail that was bowdlerized and then replaced by a running moral commentary.

In the original, for example, Lewis often described the monk (with entire accuracy) as "lustful." In the bowdlerized version the word never appears. By the canons of pure expurgation, or Bowdler's Law, its place should either have been left blank or filled in by some less offensive synonym of approximately equal moral tone. *Amorous, ardent, libidinous, sensual, wanton*—any of these might conceivably make a suitable replacement. In actual fact, the two adjectives used as substitutes are "vicious" and "glutting." Both contain an obvious judgment on sexual desire not implied in the original.

Similarly, Lewis several times spoke of Ambrosio's "incontinence," using what was then and is now the technical term for unchastity. In the bowdlerized version the word is replaced alternately by "weakness" and "infamy." It may well, of course, be infamous for a monk to be incontinent—but this was by no means implicit in the original passage.

More radical changes are to come. For example, when the climactic scenes are reached in which Ambrosio begins to lay siege to his young half-sister Antonia (of his relationship to whom, it must be said, he is entirely ignorant: he regards her simply as the pretty fifteen-year-old that she is), when these scenes are reached Lewis again employed basically neutral terminology. Ambrosio he described merely as the would-be "ravisher." As the monk's net tightened, Antonia was almost within "the grasp of the ravisher." Soon, said Lewis, she would be compelled to "comply with his desires." Not so in the bowdlerized version. Here Ambrosio is the miserable "culprit"; Antonia is almost within the grasp of the "betrayer"; soon she will "fall an easy victim to his villainy."

The last of these changes is the most important. The alteration from "comply with" to "fall victim" is a change from active to passive, from seduction-by-force to pure rape. One can guess the reason. Antonia is a favorably drawn character, one with whom the reader is intended to sympathize. But a sympathetic character, a nice girl, does not (in expurgated fiction) comply with anyone's desires. She should prefer death. Unhappily, Antonia is not able to indulge this natural preference. The plot of *The Monk* requires her temporary survival. The only way for an expurgator to follow the book at all and still preserve the reader's sympathy would be to remove the choice from Antonia's hands, by making her entirely helpless and passive and unaware. And this is what the expurgated edition proceeds to do.

In the original, Antonia was by no means unaware of what was happening. The whole force of the scene depended on her not being. As Lewis wrote it, the monk had drugged Antonia and hidden her in a catacomb for safety. His return a few hours later to go through with the actual ravishment wakes her from the trance. There is a moving and by no means indecent thousand-word passage describing her wild struggles, her prayers and supplications before finally succumbing. It is one of the several climaxes of the book. In the fourth edition these thousand words are reduced to a single sentence: "Animation was only restored to make herself sensible that the monk was a villain, and herself undone!"

Infamous villain, glutting culprit, vicious betrayer —under all these titles poor Ambrosio has been as thoroughly stigmatized as if *he* were the author of a sensational novel. And the end is not yet. The judgment on the erring monk is more explicitly stated still. Even the quotations with which Lewis began his chapters are pressed into service. The sixth chapter, for example, being mainly concerned with the original seduction of Ambrosio by the beautiful novice, had for its motto a couplet from the robustious seventeenth-century playwright Nathaniel Lee:

> While in each other's arms entranced they lay,
> They blessed the night and cursed the coming day.

Verse like this passes no judgment on anything, teaches the reader nothing useful at all. It isn't even cast in a form that can conveniently be expurgated. Consequently Maria (if it was indeed she) boldly cut it out altogether and substituted as chapter heading a little passage from Shakespeare as follows:

> "What is't ye do?"
> —"A deed without a name."

This is much more satisfactory, suggesting as it does a mystery about what goes on during seductions, a kind of nameless horror to the process that decent people don't speak of.

At any rate, the decent person who expurgated *The*

Monk doesn't speak of it. Indeed, she barely alludes to the novice's maneuvers with Ambrosio at all. In the first three editions the scene is an extended one, graphic but not pornographic, replete with clinical and amorous detail, tense with the drama of Ambrosio's impending downfall. In the bowdlerized version all this graphic prose is replaced by the brief phrase, "His vow is violated."

And then comes the most astonishing addition in the novel.

Lewis had ended *his* vow-violation chapter with a bit of dialogue: " 'Thine, ever thine,' murmured the friar, and sank upon her bosom." The sentence is, of course, one of many that were cut. The expurgator ends her chapter with a short, original interpolation—a general comment, as it were, on vow-violaters. "Tremble, Ambrosio!" the new ending reads. "The first step is taken, and he who breaks his faith with heaven will soon break it with man. Hark! 'Twas the shriek of your better angel, he flies, and leaves you for ever!"

It seems a little hard that Ambrosio's better angel should pick this crucial moment to abandon his post. Many readers of the expurgated edition have felt that a really sincere better angel would, instead of decamping, have stuck around, would have girded up his loins and got busy trying to persuade Ambrosio to do the same. In short, they have accused the better angel of being, like young Matthew Lewis, the sort who in a crisis promptly lies down.

Such criticism misses the point, however. Symbolically, the better angel's action is not only justi-

fied but necessary. For Ambrosio's companion was
not a guardian angel in the old medieval sense. He
has no place in the complicated Gothic supernatural-
ism that already existed in the novel. He is, rather, a
spirit of the coming age; the coming age will know
him as the Angel of Propriety. Where open scandal
is, he cannot live, nor can he ever, in the face of public opinion, associate with sinners. His flight from
Ambrosio marks the exact moment at which the unfortunate ecclesiastic becomes an official villain, a
man in whose fate decent people may no longer take
an interest. He is, in short, the embodied or at least
the enspirited moral of the book.

One may even speculate that on leaving Ambrosio
the better angel flew straight to Matthew Lewis. By
giving up his book, Lewis saved himself. Still only
twenty-two, truly repentant of his rashness at twenty
("high imprudence," he himself more modestly described it in a letter to his father), resolved in the
future to avail himself of the delicate tact and correct judgment possessed by his sister Maria, holding
in his delighted pocket an invitation to visit the Duke
and Duchess of Argyle at Inverary Castle, Lewis was
redeemed indeed. Within the year he and his angel
were in fit condition to sit amicably down to supper
with the fiercest bishop or the most narrow-minded
viscount in England.

The fat of the land

IT IS AN ARTICLE of faith with us Americans
that all the really soft living in colonial America was
done by visiting Englishmen. If there was one brick
house in the otherwise log-cabin capital of one of the
smaller colonies, the British governor lived in it. If
there were two, British troops got quartered in the
other one. All the wining, dancing, gaming, wench-
ing, and sumptuary dressing indulged in anywhere in
seventeenth-century America were indulged in by
visiting favorites of Charles II. We colonials stood
round in our simple homespun and watched.

An Indian I know at Cambridge named Dilip Palit
firmly believes that similar conditions prevail in India
to this very day. The English, he says, wallow in

luxury from Jodhpur to Madras. I've heard much the same thing about Singapore from a Malay Chinese in whose car I once hitchhiked a ride to London. It's an open secret, Nigerians tell me, who lives off the fat of the land *there*.

I hope all this is true, because in England itself it is we foreign students who do the soft living. As a matter of fact, Her Majesty's Government pays us to do it—or at least it splits the expenses with us. That delightful body the British Council receives perhaps a quarter of a million pounds annually for the purpose. I imagine what's involved is some sort of expiation.

Two or three summers ago, when I had first come over from New York, I decided to go up from Cambridge, where I was and am a research student, to the Edinburgh Festival. I asked my English roommate if he cared to come with me. He looked at me as if I had suggested buying a yacht.

"Me go to Edinburgh? On my grant?" he said incredulously. "I might walk to Grantchester for tea with you, provided we have it at the cheap place.

"Besides," he added, "the Festival starts in ten days. You'll never get tickets now." He had forgotten I was a foreigner.

The next morning I strolled down to the Cambridge office of the British Council. "Have you any sort of provision for sending people to the Edinburgh Festival?" I asked the girl at the desk.

"You *are* a foreign student, sir? Certainly. We can sign you up for a seven-day Festival Course. Which week would you like to go?"

"What is it going to cost?" I asked guardedly.

The girl looked slightly apologetic. "I'm afraid the Festival Course is a bit more expensive than some of the others. It's nine pounds for the week. But, of course, in addition to full board, private room, and local transportation, that includes tickets to the Glyndebourne Opera, the Old Vic, the Danish Ballet, several concerts, and the Edinburgh Tattoo; an all-day coach trip to the mountains, tea and biscuits at bedtime, complimentary membership in the International Club, and the services of two full-time counselors."

"Damn the expense," I said. "I'll go."

When I got to Edinburgh and checked in at the university residence hall where we were to be housed, I found that the British Council girl in Cambridge had understated. In addition to what she had listed, my nine pounds also entitled me to a lecture on Scottish history, a ticket to an exhibition of Gauguin, guided tours of the Castle and of Holyrood Palace, and a large glossy souvenir program marked "Price: 5 shillings."

The week was a huge success. We had bagpipes up to our ears. Glyndebourne put on a flawless performance of *The Barber of Seville*. The Nigerians, the pretty little nurses from Hong Kong, the Ghanians (Gold Coasters, they were then), the British Guianans, the four Germans, the homesick New Zealander, the other American and I all had a splendid time. I learned quite a lot about how well the English do themselves in Ghana and Guiana, and I sympathized with the plight of Germans out of whose

pockets money is plucked—or was then—to provide
luxury housing for English troops in Hamburg. I also
received from one of the full-time counselors a list
of future British Council courses.

This past Christmas I again found myself a little
low on funds—Cambridge is expensive even for foreigners—and I toyed with going on a seven-day,
seven-pound course the Council was offering in Tor-
quay. But I'm glad now I didn't. A friend of mine, a
girl from northern Italy, went, and she was badly disappointed. The nightly dances were all right, she
said; and she enjoyed the pantomime performances
and the trips to Exeter and Dartmouth. But they only
gave her one glass of wine with Christmas dinner.

The unwilling ear

I T W A S M Y R O O M M A T E who started it, with
his cheap cynicism. "Look at them," he said, curling
his lip. "Twelve guests talking to twelve bridesmaids,
and not a damn one of the twenty-four is listening.
You could go down that line telling them you'd just
blown up the Kremlin, and all they'd do is smile at
you and say, 'Yes, isn't she lovely?' "

It was the June before our senior year in college, I
was visiting his home town, these people were his
friends, not mine. I was ready to try anything. We
passed the bridal couple, and my roommate lingered
to kiss the bride. I pushed on to the maid of honor.
"I've just blown up the Kremlin," I remarked to her
chattily. She caught my tone and gave me a fraction

of her smile. "Yes, isn't she?" she said, looking with half an eye to see where the waiter with the champagne was.

"I think you've got your dress on backwards," I said to the second bridesmaid. This one must have liked me better. She flashed me a complete, luscious smile all for myself. "What did you say your name was?" she asked prettily.

"I've just drawn and quartered the Earl of Shrewsbury," I said to the ninth bridesmaid, rather loudly. The girl gave me a startled look.

"What do you expect me to do, call the police?" she asked. I was embarrassed, and I rushed on past the last three bridesmaids, muttering something about how radiant the bride was. I have a confused memory of three fixed smiles and six deaf ears, and then I lost myself in the crowd and began looking for the waiter with the champagne.

Two days later we met the girl who listened at another party. She came stealing up behind me. "You mean the police haven't got you yet?" she asked in a low, clear voice—and then my rudeness became a bond between us. "I don't think you can expect people to listen at weddings," she said. We sat down and agreed that they don't listen much anywhere else, either.

This is a pity. Good listening is one of the attributes of civilization. It is also a cultivable art, like gourmet cooking or reading Ronald Firbank. Initially it takes no more than the ability to stop talking occasionally. Then begin the subtleties, of which there are many.

I have lately been in touch with the ninth bridesmaid. She became a bride herself in the summer of 1958, after an extremely adventurous career with a radio station in Paris, and a year keeping the books for a copper mine in Arizona, but with her husband's permission we still correspond. Together she and I have worked out a sort of manual of the pleasures of listening. It divides into four parts and a bonus.

The first part is pretty obvious, especially to people who have seen *My Fair Lady*, and who were paying attention. It's simply the art of listening to what people *say*. The unwilling ear doesn't do this. It translates everything into its own pidgin English. It can tell a Western accent from a New England one, but Nebraska and Wyoming, New Hampshire and Rhode Island sound exactly alike to it. A friend of mine, the owner of such an ear, took the Boston and Maine train from New York to White River Junction, Vermont, where I met him.

"Did you have a Vermont or a Massachusetts conductor?" I asked. He didn't know. "Well, how did he announce the stations?" He just announced them, my friend said.

A living ear would have noticed a difference. Massachusetts conductors tend to assume that passengers know where they are, and make a bare announcement. If you're pulling into Greenfield, they bark, "Greenf'ld," as if it were about a syllable and a half. Vermont conductors are more suspicious of human nature, and they have perfected a cry something like a peewit's. "Greenfield!" they call, "greenfieldgreenfieldgreenfield, greeenfield." It's almost worth making the trip to hear them.

Mannerism is not all that the unwilling ear misses. It also misses shades of meaning. Really stupid ears don't even know that meaning has shades. An English poet was once standing beside a cataract (*not* the same as a waterfall—if you've an ear for shading you'll know that cataracts are bigger and make more noise than waterfalls) when a couple of tourists came strolling up for the view. Both were visibly over-whelmed by the majesty of what they saw and heard. Finally one, a man, turned to the other, a woman. "My dear," he said solemnly, "it is sublime."

"Yes," she agreed in the same awed voice, "it is nice, isn't it?"

Clearly she believed that she was saying the same thing. In this notion she was mistaken. Which puts her in the same category as a woman my ninth brides-maid knows who habitually and publicly addresses her husband as Lover, just as if James Thurber had never existed. "Come on, Lover," she'll say in ringing tones, dragging him away from a cocktail party, "we've got to take the baby sitter home." There is a theory that she thinks "lover" as a mode of address has the same meaning as "love." What her husband thinks no one quite likes to ask.

The second part of good hearing, besides hearing *what* people say, is hearing how they say it. This is the art of tone, unknown to dictionaries and courts of law. Dictionaries and courts of law have only one tone, the matter-of-fact. If it is introduced into court as evidence that the defendant was seen looking hun-grily at his fiancée and was heard to say, "I'm going to eat you alive, baby," the presumption must be that he contemplated cannibalism of a peculiarly revolting sort. His fiancée knows better. So does any student of tone.

There are not many students of tone. My ninth bridesmaid reports that her husband was talking about human frailty at a small dinner party last fall, and quoted Lope de Vega's famous prescription for it. Female infants, said Lope de Vega, should be put to death at the instant of birth. As for male infants, they are to be kept in monasteries until the age of eighteen and then sentenced to the galleys for life. "That would soon fix things up," my bridesmaid's husband concluded cheerfully.

He then became aware that his hostess was glaring at him. "You realize, of course," she said, her voice dripping scorn, "that this would mean the end of the human race in one generation?"

There was nothing for it but to mutter weakly that this aspect of the proposal had never occurred to him. "Well, it's time it did," his hostess said in firm, teacherly tones.

I myself have had similar experiences in New Hampshire. I live in a small village about fifteen miles south of the large village in which I work, and every now and then someone asks me why, when there is plenty of housing closer to hand.

The real reason is that I have been lent a ten-room farmhouse in the small village, and besides, I like the drive back and forth, which is along a river and without billboards. But occasionally this explanation bores me, and I vary it. I did about a month ago with one of my colleagues. He had asked me why I commuted

so far, and I said it was the winters—I couldn't stand
them in Hanover, they were so cold. Consequently I
had moved south to avoid them. He looked at me for
some time. "And you really think it helps?" he said
gently.

I could have answered that fifteen miles is a hun-
dredth of the way to Florida. I didn't, partly because
I didn't think of it, partly because if I had he would
unquestionably have pointed out that the difference
in winter temperature between New Hampshire and
Florida averages only some 48° Fahrenheit, and thus
that living where I do gains me less than half a degree
of warmth—say, the difference between a night at
ten below zero and one at nine and a half below. He
was a man who could listen on only one level. About
an inch down, roughly. I suspect that Lope de Vega
had friends just like him.

The third part of good listening is only for ears that
are already a bit willing, even somewhat trained.
This is the art of listening for echoes in words. Or
you could call it etymological listening. There is a
great deal of private delight to be had in it.

The prime example of the art comes neither from
me nor my ex-bridesmaid but from C. S. Lewis, the
man who wrote *The Screwtape Letters* and *Out of
the Silent Planet,* and also that book with the su-
perbly unprovocative title, *English Literature in the
Sixteenth Century, Excluding Drama.*

Apparently Professor Lewis was once introduced
to a movie star, a woman with striking beauty and no
ear for words at all. The beauty was obvious, but not
the lack of ear. Accordingly, when the man who in-

troduced them boasted that the star had "more glamour than any woman in Europe," Professor Lewis got carried away.

"Ah," he said gravely, "which is your special interest then, punctuation or sentence structure?"

"Are you kidding?" the star answered, and began to look sulky. His was no question to ask a lady.

A star with open ears (and a nodding acquaintance with etymology) would have heard the echoes in "glamour" and shared the joke. The echoes go something like this.

Back in the Middle Ages, anyone who knew how to read and write was said to possess "grammar," or a knowledge of punctuation, sentence structure, and so forth. It was not a common possession. Churchmen had grammar and read the Bible, which was fine. A few other people had grammar—and it was generally believed that what *they* read were books on sorcery, and that they spent their time casting spells. Grammar came to mean witchcraft.

The next step is that Scotsmen love to change *r*'s to *l*'s. They picked up the word "grammar" and by it they meant witchcraft, but they pronounced it with an *l*. "When devils, wizards, or jugglers deceive the sight, they are said to cast *glamour* o'er the eyes of the spectators," the Scots poet Allan Ramsay wrote in 1721.

Presently another Scots poet, finding himself hopelessly in love, complained that the girl must have been using spells. "She hauds me wi' her glamour-gift," he moaned. What Scottish girls can do, all girls can do. By the beginning of the twentieth century, any enchanting, bewitching, fascinating (Latin, *fascinare*, "to cast a spell"), or even just charming female could properly be called glamorous. Or else grammarous.

This is a fairly complicated echo, and maybe I expect too much of movie stars. Even little echoes, such as announcing checkmate in chess, and knowing that what you're really saying is the antique Persian *shah-mat*—the king is dead—add another fillip to listening.

There is a fourth and final part of the manual for alert ears, and this one is entirely the idea of my ex-bridesmaid. I'm not sure a man could have thought of it. I've contributed two or three of the examples, but even they had to be approved by her first.

This fourth art is the art of listening for WB and non-WB words. WB, I should explain, stands for well-bred. It can refer either to language or to people. Indeed, it can refer to habits. For example, it is WB in a restaurant to have the coffee brought after you are through eating, and extremely non-WB to let the waiter slop it down with your dessert, or—horrors—right with the stuffed haddock.

WB words are, of course, the equivalent of U words in England; the chief difference is that there are fewer of them. Whether this means that there are fewer well-bred people in America than there are upper-class ones in England, neither my bridesmaid nor I care to guess. We simply report that of WB words there are a mere handful.

Without allowing what I hope is a moderately WB essay to degenerate into a vulgar quiz, I propose to list some of that handful in such a way as to give willing ears a little practice right now. Take, to begin, a woman who is admiring two pieces of cloth which hang down on either side of a friend's window. "My," she exclaims, "what lovely _____!"

"Curtains," she exclaims, if she's WB. If the pieces of cloth are long and made of heavy material, she might perhaps call them draperies. But if she says "drapes," she has branded herself a non-WB.

Now suppose this same woman later discloses plans to change her residence. "Jack and I," she tells her bridge club, "are about to build a new _____." "House," of course, if she's WB; "home" if she's not.

When the new structure is completed, the woman and her husband invite about sixty of their friends to come for a housewarming. (Non-WB's have the gang over for a homewarming, I imagine.) Most of the sixty bring small objects with them, and on seeing these the woman's eyes light up. "Oh," she says happily, "I do like getting _____."

"Presents" is the WB, "gifts" the non-WB. This doesn't mean that the word "gift" has no place in the language at all. "Gift-wrapped" seems to be correct enough, though hardly WB; and even Gift Shoppes may have some function in a corrupt society. But things given to friends are presents.

I should have mentioned that the couple we've been talking about served rum punch at their housewarming, and that their punchbowl was grossly inadequate for serving sixty-two people. They had to borrow a larger one from a cousin of Jack's, and it was Jack who telephoned. "Say, Peggy, I was won-

dering if you'd ———— us your punchbowl," he asked
in his rough way. "Lend," Jack said, if he was WB,
"loan" if he wasn't. I hope he said lend. It would put
him, in this respect, in a class with Shakespeare.
"Friends, Romans, countrymen, lend me your ears,"
requested Shakespeare's well-bred character Mark
Antony. Probably if Antony had coarsely used "loan,"
the citizens of Rome would have refused, there'd
have been no speech, no civil war or battle at
Philippi, and very likely no Roman Empire for Gib-
bon to describe the decline and fall of.

I've saved WB pronunciation for last. So far as I am
aware, there's very little of it. A word like "either,"
for example, proves nothing. Some WB's say ee-ther,
some say eye-ther. Some address the sisters of their
parents as ahnt, some as ant. It is pure bunk about
society saying Marie. But there is one infallible test.
Listen to someone ask for a bacon, lettuce, and
———— sandwich. If there's an *ah* in tomato, the
asker is purest WB. If there's an *a*, he's a lout. Indeed, I have heard an aristocrat defined as someone
whose family has said tomahto for three generations.
I'm not claiming it *matters* whether a man is an aristocrat, only that if one happens to meet his grand-
parents over a tossed salad it is absurdly easy to find
out.

Thus end the four parts of the manual of hearing.
Now for the bonus, which is overhearing. Overhearing is maybe the keenest pleasure of all, but it has a
code of ethics without which it lapses into eaves-
dropping, a non-WB practice. The code is simply that
anything you get in a public place is fair game, any-

thing in a private place is out. As usual, it is my bridesmaid who has got the prize example.

When she was working on that radio station in Paris, she used to go to the Opéra nearly every week. Sometimes she went with Frenchmen, sometimes with Americans. Occasionally she went alone, for better listening—to opera and audience both. It was after one of these alone evenings that going out she heard unmistakably American voices ahead of her (Indiana or Illinois, she thinks), and spotted two middle-aged men in dacron suits. Presumably they were in town for a business convention and had somehow wandered off to that splendid opera house. She could hardly wait to get their spontaneous impression of *La Forza del Destino,* and craftily trailed them down three flights of marble stairs. Alas, they had fallen silent. Neither spoke another word until they were almost to the street. Then the tall one turned gravely to the short one. "In a building this size, you'd think they'd install elevators," he said.

As long as human vocal cords hold out, wherever two or three are gathered together there will be similar delights awaiting the open ear. All it takes is listening.

The Henry James papers

WHEN I FIRST MATRICULATED at Cambridge University as a graduate research student, some six and a half years ago, I knew exactly what I intended to study. I intended to study the later novels of Henry James there in England, where he wrote them. By a profound analysis of his style, I was going to settle once and for all, I hoped, the long-argued question of whether James in his last years was an old master or an old impostor.

In this ambitious plan I was not alone. At a conservative estimate, at least two hundred other young Americans, not to mention several Englishmen and a stray European or so, were at that moment also taking notes on *The Ambassadors* and *The Golden Bowl*, and planning their doctoral dissertations on the later works of James. The number has since increased. A friend of mine who sits on the Degree Committee of the Faculty of English at Cambridge told me recently that in my time, out of all the prospective research students in literature, only one in twenty wanted to do his thesis on Henry James. Now, he says, it's about one in six, including practically *all* of the Americans who apply. To borrow (a scholar's privilege) the phrase of Stephen Potter, James is very likely the most O.K. author of the twentieth century. It's a kind of distinction to have studied him even if you didn't learn anything.

Six years ago, of course, I had no idea that the competition for James was so severe. I was simply another full-grown but wide-eyed American—intoxicated with literature, proud that my country had produced a novelist as complex and subtle and widely admired in Europe as Henry James, and eager to associate myself with this towering figure on any terms. It was only gradually, during my first few months at Cambridge, that I discovered how many associates James already had.

There was F. O. Matthiessen, who had taken the later novels (*my* novels) and written a definitive book on them called *Henry James: The Major Phase*. There was young Michael Swan, right there in England, who had made his attachment to James before he was twenty-five. (I was already twenty-five.) There was Leon Edel, the brilliant professor at New York University, who knew all about James's life, far more than James seems to have been aware of himself, and who had written or edited five books on the great man and his work. (I had written one slim "appreciation.") There was F. W. Dupee, who knew all about James's life, too, and who had written or edited three books. There was Simon Nowell-Smith, of London, who had written prefaces and whose specialty was collecting literary anecdotes about James. There was Gerard Hopkins, nephew of the poet and master analyst of James's style. And these were only the great ones. In a card file I still own, I've got listed eighty-two learned articles, by eighty-two Ph.D.s, on the subject of James's late novels alone, and my list is far from complete.

I was horribly discouraged as I slowly became aware of all this. The further I got into James, the less I could find that there was left to write. My supervisor wasn't much help, either. "Come see me when you've finished your first chapter," he told me at our first interview. "I can't do anything for you until then. James is not, I rejoice to say, one of my specialties." Seeing my depressed face, he added, more kindly, "Even if he were, I couldn't possibly find you a topic. Not in this era of mass scholarship. Finding some new trifle to write about is two-thirds of your job as a research student." And he gave me a glass of sherry.

A good many people were giving me glasses of sherry that term, which is one of the pleasures of being *in statu pupillari* at Cambridge. The senior tutor of my college did even better. He invited me to his house for midday dinner one Sunday in December, just after Michaelmas Term ended. Naturally, we had a glass of sherry before sitting down.

"Well, Perrin," he said, handing me my glass, "how are you getting on? Work going all right?"

"Actually, not quite so well as I could wish, sir," I answered bravely, meaning that it was not going at all, and flattering myself that in this restrained phrase I was catching the authentic English note.

"I think someone told me you're doing a dissertation on Henry James?"

"Yes, sir."

The senior tutor lit his pipe, using a match the size of a small chair leg. "I used to know James when I was a boy," he said, in a tone that was either really off-handed or an excellent simulacrum of offhandedness. Not being able to decide which, I played my answer safe.

"Golly, sir, I envy you," I, as Henry James would have put it, humorously wailed.

The senior tutor looked pleased. "Yes, he was a great friend of an aunt of mine in London. Sometimes, when I stayed with her during school holidays, he'd be there, too. I remember once, when I was about fifteen, having to walk with him down to the post office. He talked the whole way, and I didn't understand a word he said. Funny fellow."

"But a *brilliant* novelist, sir."

"That's a portrait of my aunt," the senior tutor went on, nodding at a painting over the fireplace. "She was very good to me when I was a boy."

I think I would have recognized the painting as a Sargent even if its subject's nephew hadn't promptly volunteered the information. I looked with considerable interest at the little gray woman whom Sargent had painted. But I couldn't help thinking that we were getting pretty remote from revelations about Henry James.

The senior tutor was watching my reactions in a penetrating, head-bent way he had, and now he proceeded. "You know," he said, "my aunt lived to be almost eighty, and when she died, I was her sole heir."

I didn't see myself saying "Congratulations, sir," so I said nothing. He lit his pipe with another enormous match and proceeded. "I went through her papers after she died, in 1937, and among the rest I found a bundle of letters from Henry James. She was a great saver."

"My God, sir, how wonderful! What did you do with them?" I, as the master would say, all but panted.

The senior tutor puffed away. "Why, nothing in particular. My wife and I read a few of the letters at the time, but they appeared to be purely domestic in their scope, and then the war came along and we rather forgot about them. But your coming to lunch somehow put my wife in mind of them, and this morning she went up to the boxroom and found them. There seem to be more than I had remembered."

He picked up a shoe box from a window seat, where I hadn't even noticed it, and handed it to me. "Glance at them, if you like," he said, and strolled off to give his wife a hand with dinner.

I stood goggling after him for a minute. Then, with an almost sacramental gesture, I opened the shoe box, which was a heavy one, and looked inside. It was stuffed neatly but tightly with substantial-looking letters tied in packets of about ten. One of these I tugged out and untied. I took the top letter out of its envelope and gently unfolded it. It was dated, in a hand that I had seen often enough in facsimile, "Lamb House, Rye, Jan. 12th, 1912." I started reading.

"DEAR FANNY [it began]: I take the Sunday p.m. train up . . . and am due at Victoria at 6:55. I shall want above all after my grimmish Joannine fortnight, immediate Conversation, and should I find you—the purest font of it in all the great town—were I to come to you that very same Sunday evening, the 14th? If not, we will cast about —but I shall be so fresh at that first ecstatic hour."

In this, I recognized the authentic note of the Henry James who once went out to dinner a hundred and seven times during a single winter. Even if I hadn't, the letter was signed, "Ever your old H.J."

People always seem to describe their mental states in terms of physical reactions: sinking feelings in their stomachs, tensings of their spines, tinglings in their scalps. My reaction to this, one of the two or three profoundly ecstatic experiences of my life, was a near-cessation of physical activity. I could hardly taste my food when we sat down to dinner, and would much have preferred not to eat it. I will swear that my eyes took in less light and my ears less sound than normal. The senior tutor seemed to be talking at me from some considerable distance. But I listened intently.

"Well, Perrin," he asked, when he had finished carving, "do you think these letters would really have any interest? My wife feels they do, but on the whole I incline to disagree with her."

"Oh, *yes,* sir," I said, hoping I wasn't shouting. "Those letters have a great deal of interest. I think they're clearly publishable, and I suspect they're also salable. Henry James is an awfully important author."

The senior tutor looked dubious. "I don't believe I'd care to sell them," he said. "Nor do I quite see why anyone would want to publish them. After all, who on earth would read that sort of thing?"

So I told him about a little book *I'd* read, called *Three Letters From Henry James to Joseph Conrad,* published in London, in 1926. Lest he object that his aunt wasn't Joseph Conrad, I hurried on to tell him about *Letters of Henry James to Walter Berry,* published by Caresse Crosby at the Black Sun Press, in Paris, in 1928. I mentioned *Henry James: Letters to A. C. Benson and Auguste Monod,* brought out in London by Elkin Mathews, and in New York by Scribner's, in 1930. I artfully referred to a magazine article I'd read just a couple of weeks before, called "An Unpublished Letter of Henry James." (It was a letter to an actress named Marion Terry, and not at all epochal.) If it had been in existence at the time, I would have cited, item by item, Leon Edel's definitive list of a hundred and seventy-two books, pamphlets, and magazine articles that print one or more previously unknown James letters and that derive some or all of their *raison d'être* from that fact.

"This is all very interesting," the senior tutor said when I finally ran out of breath. "Incredible, to be quite honest. But I shall think most seriously about what you have told me."

"Would you be willing to let me read the letters meanwhile?" I asked, as casually as I could manage. "Whatever happens to them, they ought to be sorted and catalogued, and I would count it an honor to do so."

"Mm, I see no harm in that."

"In fact, we were hoping you'd want to," his wife added. "I think my husband's aunt was a more distinguished woman than he seems to realize, and these letters may well have some historical interest." She smiled at me in a friendly way. "You must let me give you tea when you come over to work on them."

Of course I pranced away in wild academic glee, full of Brussels sprouts and custard tart though I was. I could already see the little book or, at any rate, the very long article that would result from my editing of the letters, and my consequent assured place in the Jamesian bibliography. With enough footnotes, the letters might make do as my actual dissertation, as well. And phrases like "grimmish Joannine fortnight" just naturally engender footnotes—good solid ones that do not stop with identifying Joanne and dating the fortnight but that go on to explain, with some bits of what we academics call *facetiae*, what was so grim about it and her.

There would be pages and pages of such footnotes.

I could see them all. Leaving out the unfortunate
Joanne, I'd already found in the few letters I'd had
time to look through: (1) a ribald remark about a
woman, apparently of social prominence, named
Ottoline, (2) a mild dig at Hugh Walpole, (3) two
references to a mysterious Constance F., alias "our
Gorgeous and Glorious one," and (4) a dog known as
"the awful Albino monster." I could have written a
footnote about *him* then and there, as I walked back
to college.

It is, indeed, this kind of elaborate documentation
that we scholars love best. The typical Ph.D. candidate doesn't have daydreams of working out a
neocritical theory that will account for the morbid
element in John Donne's shorter lyrics (hardly a scholarly thing to work out, at best); he dreams of discovering Chaucer's will in some old records office,
and publishing it (one page of will and two hundred
pages of notes), or of stumbling on an unedited manuscript of Marlowe's in a castle loft, and editing it.
Such activity is certain not only to produce a book
but a book that will be talked about and reviewed
and even read, a book that will require a lovely long
delicious preface by the scholar himself. Scholarship,
at least literary scholarship. is essentially parasitic,
and suitable hosts have been in short supply for a
long time.

The next day, humming like an Aëdes mosquito, I
set joyously to work, counting the letters and arrang-
ing them chronologically. It was exciting work. I
made an important discovery almost at once. My
senior tutor's aunt, I found, had kept the letters in

their original envelopes, of which there were some ninety, bearing postmarks from 1906 up to within a couple of months of James's death, in 1916. This fact had, naturally enough, led the senior tutor and his wife to suppose that there were also about ninety letters. But I soon discovered that, beginning around 1910, his aunt had taken to stuffing several letters in one envelope, and there were actually a total of a hundred and thirty-four holograph letters. I could, at that point, have safely vanished with forty-four of them (worth, apart from their literary value, between ten and twenty-five dollars apiece on the open market), and I even considered doing so; but of course I hoped, in due time, to be allowed to depart with the whole collection, and so put the idea by as unworthy.

Instead, I worked happily away on the catalogue, finding ever more references to Constance F., the Gorgeous and Glorious one, and I continued, on the occasional days that my senior tutor came home for tea, to impress on him the urgency of getting the letters into print. Once, I remember, when I was suggesting that publication would be only fair to his aunt, he ducked his head in annoyance. "They are, after all, private letters, Perrin," he said. "I'm not sure that I am not betraying my aunt's trust in even letting you read them. 'Significant,' or not, they perhaps ought to be burned." I said no more about what his aunt would have wished.

A couple of days later, however, I managed to get hold of my supervisor, out of term though it was, and even though I still had no first chapter of a thesis to show him. Up until then, I had confided in no one about the letters, fearing that news of them would bring swarms of hungry scholars buzzing up from London and Oxford to snatch them from me. But to my supervisor I told the full story, which he followed with open, almost drooling mouth, and then I asked him how I should proceed.

"I know your senior tutor only in the most casual way," he said. "But I do know that he's a scholar of the old school. I shouldn't push him, if I were you. In the first place, it's hard for him to believe that anything so recent really matters. If the letters were from Herodotus, or even Milton, he could see their importance at once. But a mere novelist who flourished during his own lifetime—that's another matter. Secondly, Perrin, if he *should* become convinced of their interest, there's no real reason why he should give them to you. He might well decide to edit them himself. Or he might prefer to turn them over to someone who has, shall we say, a somewhat more durable connection with the University."

"In other words, there's no hope for me at all," I blurted, sinking at once into despair. It crossed my mind that I had picked a poor confidant. An active supervisor in his forties can always *make* James one of his specialties.

"Of course there's hope for you," the supervisor said reassuringly. "I simply mean that you must give the man time to digest the idea that there is another Henry James besides the stammering old bore he remembers. We digest slowly in Cambridge. I think he may very well give them to you in the end." He smiled. "After all, they've been waiting for you twenty years, just like Sleeping Beauty. Have a glass of sherry."

Chastened, a little suspicious but still hopeful, I went back to my cataloguing, which I finished a few days before Christmas. The day after it was done, I had a conference with the senior tutor in his office at college. As a thank-you present for all the tea, I took him a copy of Elizabeth Robins' *Theatre and Friendship*, a plump volume subtitled "Some Henry James Letters." He barely glanced at it, thus wasting my ingenuity in getting hold of the second, or Popular, edition.

"Perrin," he said, "I've discussed the problem of these wretched letters with one or two Fellows of the college. They feel, as I do, that it would be rash to proceed without further information. One of them has agreed to make inquiries for me in London. Perhaps you had better come see me again about the middle of next term."

"Yes, sir," I said.

Unable to contemplate the idea of two months' steady waiting, I left Cambridge the same week, bound for the Continent with some cousins, and eventually wound up spending a grimmish solitary fortnight in Marseilles. My dreams were troubled with visions of footnotes, all by me, and book reviews, all favorable.

It was no better when I came back to Cambridge, at the beginning of Lent Term. By day, I forced myself to sit in the English Faculty Library taking notes on scholarly works about James, and at night I continued to dream. When I had taken notes on about forty books and something over three hundred learned articles, I presented myself in the senior tutor's office again, a trifle haggard and twisting a hypothetical cap in my hands.

He stood up as I came in, which was a bad sign. He always did that when he wanted you to leave quickly. "Perrin, I'm sorry about this," he said. "Those letters turn out to be of some considerable interest. I can still hardly credit the report. If I do anything with them—and I have not yet made up my mind—I'm afraid I shall have to call on someone with greater experience than your own. But my wife agrees with me that you must feel free to quote them in your dissertation. There would even be no objection to your quoting an entire letter. I'm sorry we can't do any better than that."

I had learned long ago that the senior tutor was not a man with whom you plead, and I didn't try pleading now. I went back to my rooms and gave myself four glasses of sherry (all I had), and felt sad and rather noble about the forty-four letters I'd refrained from taking. What the senior tutor really meant, I decided, was that he didn't care to give these English letters to a brash visiting American who would bear them off in triumph to New York and probably wind up presenting them to Columbia. And I didn't really blame him. The situation was itself so Jamesian—all he really needed was a homely niece whom I should have had to marry in order to gain possession—that I couldn't but understand. I wondered sadly if my supervisor would get them in the end (and if he would have the nerve to tell me), or whether it would be the man who did the inquiring in London.

At the end of the Easter Term, it was myself I bore off to New York, grant run out and dissertation not even begun. Two years passed before I finally found a little morsel of James not yet so chewed over by learned teeth that I couldn't gnaw one more sliver of scholarship out. I thought about the senior tutor's aunt's letters only on rare occasions, when I wanted to feel sad and noble.

Then, a couple of years ago, I went back to Cambridge to write my long-delayed dissertation. Practically my first social engagement was the senior tutor's annual sherry party for new and returned students.

"Well, Perrin," he greeted me. "It's good to see you back. Get yourself some sherry."

I did, and he followed me over to the sideboard. "Do you remember those letters of my aunt's that you catalogued?" he asked.

I nodded dumbly.

"They've gone to America," he said, laughing as if it were some kind of joke between us. "Leon Edel—do you know him?—has carried them off to New York. I believe he's considering them for a new collective edition he has in—ah—'the works.' Your countrymen are certainly tireless scholars, ha-ha."

It's not the ending Henry James would have used. But then James was not a very good scholar. As a matter of fact, he wasn't even a college man.

Ah, New Hampshire

OLD MRS. HALKS, who lives about half a mile from where I do in central New Hampshire, has a saying about the fatal attraction of the soil hereabouts. "The land kind o' reaches up and grabs ye," she says, "and 'twon't let go."

When I look around the township two of whose twelve hundred residents we are, I am forced to agree. Since the Halkses and the Spencers arrived in 1729, the land doesn't seem to have let go of anything. The two-room clapboard house erected by Henry Spencer in 1734, for example, stands by the Center Brook yet; these days it's the village library. An old barn they say Henry and his sons put up around 1740 is both standing and still in service. It's part of a three-barn complex used by my neighbor Alf Martineau to house his cows, his hay, and his dried citrus pulp. (He imports about forty tons a year from Florida for the cows.) I have a feeling that if you looked in the long grass beside the door, you could still find one of Henry Spencer's old hand-forged scythes, a bit rusty, perhaps, but protected and preserved and firmly held in its place by a chunk of our local granite. I know you'll find Henry Spencer himself, kept down by a larger piece of that same granite, over in the Center graveyard.

What really strikes me as remarkable, though, is the way the land can take a moving object and bring it to a halt. I'm not talking about the row of old Plymouths gradually growing into the soil behind Martineau's barn. I'm talking about the bright new trailers that swing carelessly down Route Eight, reach our neighborhood, and suddenly get trapped onto cement-block foundations. The township is full of these marooned wanderers. I would guess we have at least thirty-five, beached like whales along the township roads. A tenth of our population lives in them. Another tenth has plans.

It is said that other parts of the country are rich in trailers, too. Mr. Martineau, who not only imports feed from Florida, but who has been down there himself, reports that the whole state is dotted with trailer parks and that every day you can see great pink-and-chromium houses roll in behind cars with Ohio license plates and hook up for the winter. But these are mere fleeting visitors. Come April they are due back in Ohio, and they trundle northward with mobility unimpaired—the modern gypsies of the Middle West. I think it is mainly here in New England that young trailers which have scarcely traveled fifty miles from the factory pluck off their wheels and settle down to become permanent parts of the landscape. It is an odd experience to watch them do it.

Still, I have to whether I like it or not. Between here and the Halks place, which I pass every day on my way to work, there are three of these monstrous settlers, in varying states of permanence. One, which arrived only last fall, is right across the road from the old house. It belongs to young Stephen Halks, who came home from a Long Island airplane factory last year with his new wife. The young couple haven't even had time to strip the tires off their house, but they have got the weight of it resting on concrete blocks, and they've built a picket fence all the way around, either to keep the baby in or (more likely) to make sure the whole caboodle doesn't run away with some passing Buick from Massachusetts. Next summer, Mrs. Halks says, they're going to get a proper granite base under her for sure.

The second trailer, a bright orange one with streamlined fittings, is only just around the corner from where I live. It belongs to a bachelor farmer named Roy Chipman. His previous dwelling, a quite beautiful Dutch colonial house built by a Spencer in the 1820's, burned three years ago, and Roy bought the trailer as a substitute. For a full year no one was sure whether he meant to stay up here in New Hampshire or move south, because all he did was roll his new house in about twenty feet from the town road and hook up a makeshift pump to the well. That fall when it got cold he stuck a rusty kerosene barrel on the back. (Roy doesn't hold with bottled gas.) But in the spring of 1958 he apparently came to some sort of decision. He laid a fieldstone foundation that ought to last two hundred years, and got his brother to help him mount the trailer on it. In odd moments during the summer he stretched an orange-and-green canvas awning all along the front, and he built a surprisingly trim toolshed onto the end that was designed to be hitched to cars. Just beyond that he's got his vegetable patch. What future improvements he intends, I don't know. Roy confides neither in Mrs. Halks nor in me.

I come now to the showpiece of our road, the real proof of what a New Englander can do with a trailer when he puts his mind on it. I'm speaking of the mobile home in which live the Boals, father, mother, and two children. The Boal mobile home is a securer part of our landscape than Mount Monadnock. Mr. Boal brought her in nearly ten years ago, and he's been anchoring her down and tying her closer to the soil ever since. Where Roy has that little toolshed, Boal has got a two-car garage attached, complete with a poured concrete floor. The four big doors are painted a glinty cobalt blue to match the exterior of the trailer. Running clear over the entire structure and extending out six inches on each side he has a second roof of asphalt shingles, built to last. She'll never weather out. He has a granite walk going up to her from the road, and an extra outer wall at the end opposite the garage, and a cobalt-blue trellis all along the back. He's even added a copper gutter with a downspout. All you can see of the actual trailer any more is the shimmering cobalt-blue and chromium front, which I am sure Mrs. Boal simonizes spring and fall. Anything securer from the ravages of time I have never met, except once in a cemetery in Scotland. There about every third tomb had in front of it a bowl of flowers, placed there sometime in the nineteenth century. All the flowers were identical, and all were made out of painted porcelain and wire, since flowers made of leaves and petals are known to fade. Over each porcelain bouquet was a large glass bell jar to keep the rain off. Over each bell jar was a wire cage to keep it from getting broken. You could just dimly make out the flowers, far inside.

I, alas, won't be here to see it, because I am made of frail flesh and blood, and I am beginning to weather already. But I know what New Hampshire is going to look like next century. Mount Monadnock will be an inch or so down. If we have war or really determined quarrying, it may be many feet lower. Most of the remaining clapboard houses will be gone, since what the termites miss fire will get. But chromium is incorruptible. Scattered over our valleys, winking in the sunlight, will be ten thousand thousand bright-hued, hideous lumps, each an immortal trailer, each looking as aboriginal and as immovable as the dolmens at Stonehenge. Ah, progress! Ah, New Hampshire!

Don't give me one dozen roses, give me a nosegay

IT IS WELL KNOWN that when two or three animals of the same breed are gathered together, a special name applies. And so with birds of a feather. A flock of geese in the barnyard is a gaggle, and a flight of wild geese in the sky is a skein. Everyone knows that, just as everyone knows that three elk make a gang. Even dim old ladies like my Great-aunt Alexandra know this sort of thing, as I once discovered to my cost.

"That's a fine clowder of cats you have, Aunt Alex," I told the old dowager one day when I was bringing her some peanut brittle from my mother.

She gazed fondly down at the five sleek tabbies with whom, at that time, she shared her apartment.

"Ah," she said musingly. "It seems only yesterday that they were a mere kindle of kittens."

"If you let them get any fatter," I retorted, nettled, "they'll look like a pride of lions."

"You'll be calling them a pod of whales next," she snapped.

I could think of no better answer than retreat. As quietly as if I were practicing to join a sleuth of bears, I crept out the door and went on home, eventually winding up in the garage, where I consoled myself with a fesnyng of pet ferrets I then kept. Zoological terminology is all too widely known.

It is by no means so generally known, however, that clusters of things and of people have their special names just as clusters of animals do. I didn't know it myself until recently, when I came into possession of a late-Victorian dictionary. Indeed, there is a lot I didn't know until then. Late-Victorian dictionaries are veritable treasurehouses of the elegant and the esoteric. They are especially sound on the finer points of linguistic etiquette and on the British pronunciation of names, whether place or sur. I have learned from mine, for example—*Nuttall's Standard Dictionary of the English Language* ("based on the labours of the most Eminent Lexicographers"), published in London in 1887—how to deal with upper-class names like Taliaferro (you pronounce it, of course, *tol*-i-ver), Foljambe (*fool*-jam), and Urquhart-Beaulieu (urk-*wart*—*bew*-lee). I have memorized a goodly list of elegant foreign phrases, together with some hints on when it is *de rigueur*, as we say, to use them. I feel that I am now conversant with the correct, upper-class word for just about every conceivable situation. I am drunk with Victorian multiples.

Someday I am going to take a walk, preferably in Italy, through one of those crowded landscapes like a medieval painting, with some poor fool who doesn't own a late-Victorian dictionary and who has not the slightest idea of what is *ben trovato,* or even *convenable.* The scene will be a country road on a little hill overlooking a harbor, and the conversation will go like this:

POOR FOOL: Hey, look at that old biddy with all the sticks on her back. That's the biggest load of sticks I ever saw.

ME: Biddy? Load of sticks? Oh, you mean that old peasant woman climbing the hill with the *faggot*? It is large, isn't it? I believe the old creature must be carrying quite two hundred sticks.

POOR FOOL: And look behind her—all those priests! There's a regular flock of them. Say, what's cooking?

ME: Why, I should judge that this assemblage of clergy forms the advance guard, as it were, of a religious procession. Today is the feast—or, as we say, the *festa*—of St. Catherine.

POOR FOOL: I'll say it's a *festa*! Look, here comes a whole slew of minstrels. What's that second gang of them playing? It looks as if they had miniature harps.

ME: They *do* have miniature harps. This is the first troupe of minstrels I recall having seen that included a melody of harpers. As my musical friend Eddie Burghersh-Tyrwhitt would soon tell you, it's a most irregular arrangement. For my part, I find it *un peu vulgaire.*

POOR FOOL: Where do you suppose they're headed for? Up to that old monastery we passed, with all the holy Joes standing around in the court-yard?

ME: Oh, come now, I should hardly say the mon-astery houses a community of saints. *Au contraire.* To my notion, these medieval monastics are more likely to be a pack of rascals, if not an actual gang of thieves. Read Sainte-Beuve. But look out in the har-bor, past that group, or chain, of islands. Don't I descry a vessel of some sort?

POOR FOOL: A vessel? You blind or something? There's a whole parcel of sailboats, if that's what you mean. And there's a lot of people swimming in front of the boats.

ME: You have got sharp eyes. I had better take out my glasses. (*I remove a pair of old-fashioned opera glasses from my rucksack and study the harbor through them.*) Yes, I do now perceive that there is what might properly be described as a flotilla of sail. And I am able to perceive that, as you stated, it is preceded by a water-polo seven. No doubt they are harbor folk coming to join the festival.

POOR FOOL: Here, let me have those glasses. I just saw a man in a green jacket duck into that bunch of trees on the second island.

ME (*retaining the opera glasses*): There is no such thing as a "bunch" of trees. What you mean is a stand, or grove, unless there are enough of them to be called a small wood, in which case they are a spinney. I should myself, however, denominate the growth on the second island as mere boscage.

POOR FOOL: Well, whatever it is, there're two men in green jerkins in it.

ME: My dear fellow, there are four. Beyond question they constitute a stalk of foresters. I foresee some stirring scene of the chase.

POOR FOOL: Buster, you're wrong. Those men are in there picking flowers. I bet they're going to decorate the sailboats with them.

ME (*coldly*): I fail to discern a single nosegay. Ah, now I have it—if you look closely, you will observe that they are superintending a muster of peacocks. Rather fine ones, too. *They* are intended for the procession, unquestionably. Yes, I see that the leading craft has paused to embark them.

POOR FOOL: If you aren't going to let me look through the glasses, they can embark the whole damned boscage, as far as I'm concerned—I've had it. Besides, I'm hungry. *J'ai faim.* You don't happen to have a serving of sandwiches in your sack there? Or maybe a clutch of eggs, a rope of onions, or a mash of potatoes?

ME (*impressed in spite of myself*): What do you take me for—a purveyor of viands? A kind of mobile Fortnum & Mason? I am as empty-handed as yourself, now that I have replaced the glasses in the rucksack. Yet I, too, feel the pangs of hunger. Let us hasten to the *piazza* of yonder village and purchase —let me see— a caste of bread, a flitch or so of smoked halibut, and perhaps a stoup of wine. *Mio bimbo,* we'll fall on it like an horde of savages.

Eximus, left, as a lacrosse twelve enters from the right, bearing a bench of bishops on its shoulders. A peal of bells is heard in the distance, a knot of toads leaps frantically from under the twelve's feet, and as, high above, an exaltation of larks breaks into song, the curtain falls.

The service in Union Square

NOBODY WEARS A COAT in Union Square, not
on summer afternoons. The sun is far too hot, and
you'd bake in your jacket like a potato. But I was
waiting for a party to begin, and I came into the park
respectably clad in a dark business suit and tie. I
found a shady bench free of shirt-sleeved old men,
and sat down to read the science fiction magazine I'd
bought in Grand Central. On both sides of me the
old men went on with their chess and checkers.

For perhaps ten minutes I read undisturbed. My
mind was off on the far side of an alien galaxy, and
I was totally unconscious of Union Square. My nose,
to be sure, had begun to report the immediate presence of whisky fumes, but I read serenely on.

Then a voice mumbled at my ear. I roused myself, and the mumbling resolved into words. "Do you believe in this here Astrology?" the voice asked.

I turned my head, getting the full broadside of alcohol, and saw a little red-faced Irishman sitting next to me. He, too, had a coat, though it rested on the bench beside him.

"Well, it's pretty hard to tell about these things," I answered guardedly, not knowing much about astrology.

The little Irishman lifted his eyes from the cover of my magazine (which showed the planet Saturn in three colors) and peered at the sky. He raised one knobby hand in a sweeping gesture. "I mean, do you believe in all that up there? Religion, Astrology, it's all the same."

"You've got to believe in something," I answered. I was twenty-two, if that's any excuse.

"Oh, God, if I only could."

"Well, can't you?"

"All my life I've been searching," the Irishman said huskily. "You're a student; you've read all them books. Tell me, Mister, what is the Truth?"

I thought of jesting Pilate, but this man was deadly earnest. Before I could deliver a safe platitude on truth, he suddenly looked me in the eye, and his face was wet with tears. "You're a scholar at the seminary, I can tell by looking," he declared. "Please, sir, what's the Truth of it all?"

I began to regret wearing my charcoal-gray suit. This man was drunk, but he was not to be put off with light answers, and he was obviously determined to delve into theology, with me in the role of epistemological expert. In desperation, I asked him to tell me about his life.

His name was Joseph Donnelly, he was forty-six years old, and he had been, he said, a fighter in Madison Square Garden. But whisky had undone him. He had tried Alcoholics Anonymous; he had tried everything, and nowhere had he found help. He did have a brother, however, a bank examiner in Trenton, New Jersey, and the brother might be persuaded to take him in. Did I think he should go to his brother in Trenton?

At last I understood. Joe had made his pitch, very roundabout, but a clear pitch. My party had started twenty minutes back, and I was glad of a chance to escape. I stood up.

"Mr. Donnelly," I said, and he nodded delightedly.

"Yes, Reverend. Yes, that's my name."

"Mr. Donnelly, I've really got to be going. But I wish you'd let me make a little contribution to your railroad fare."

Joe's eyes filled with tears again, and he reached in his pocket. To my utter amazement, he pulled out a brand-new five-dollar bill and a whole palmful of silver.

"You thought I was a bum," he said thickly.

I had thought exactly that, and I was ashamed. My only salvation was to act out the clergyman's part he had assigned me.

"Well," I continued boldly, "then let me pray for you."

"And would you do that, Your Reverence?"

I nodded, feeling a fool, and held out my hand to say good-by. That was a mistake. He caught my hand up and kissed it, quite dramatically, as though I were a bishop. I could feel a purple flush beginning to creep up both over my face and over the vest I wasn't wearing. But there was no turning back now. Joe was waiting expectantly. I raised my newly kissed hand.

"The Lord bless you and keep you, the Lord make his face to shine upon you, the Lord lead you to him," I gabbled as fast as I could. Snatching up my magazine, I hurried from the park. A subdued cheer from the other benches followed me, and in spite of the terrible heat, I crossed Fourteenth Street in an undignified clerical run.

The year of the dog

THAT THE ENGLISH have a weakness for dogs, no reasonable man could deny. Dogs live well in England. They are cosseted, spoiled, and sometimes made to wear boots on rainy days. But to claim, as some do, that the contemporary British dog receives more attention and enjoys more privileges than any other dog has ever received or enjoyed—this is absurd. If I were a dog, I should choose to be born not in twentieth-century England but in seventeenth-century Japan. So would any sensible animal.

After all, at this very minute there are thousands of dogs in Great Britain without a home to call their own. But a Japanese dog of the 1690's, on finding himself homeless, could move into one of the Government dog hostels. Many a dog in England will go supperless to bed tonight—or at least he could have eaten another helping if pressed. But Japanese dogs from 1694 onwards received a generous Government ration. Indeed, by 1696 the purchase of dog food was taking slightly over five per cent of the Japanese Government's total revenue.

In Great Britain it remains lawful to aim a vengeful kick at a dog which has just bitten your ankle, or even at one which merely seems to be contemplating this action. In Japan, in 1698, about five hundred people were sent to prison for kicking dogs. Most of them remained there for the next eleven years.

It all began because His Highness the Prince Tsunayoshi, fifth shogun of the Tokugawa line and feudal ruler of Japan, was born in 1646, otherwise known as the Year of the Dog. At the time the fact seems to have made little impression on him, and until the prince's forty-first year he was better known for his interest in Buddhist theology than for his devotion to animals. But in 1687 a new day dawned for the dogs of Japan. Prince Tsunayoshi had been alarmed for some years over his inability, even with the aid of several dozen concubines, to produce an heir to the shogunate. Fertility rites had been of no avail; sacrifices to Buddha had produced nothing; artificial insemination had not been invented.

Then a Buddhist priest named Ryuko, the prince's personal confessor, got an inspiration. Tsunayoshi's patron saint, so to speak, was the dog; yet heretofore the shogun had done absolutely nothing for dogs, had in fact watched unmoved while his samurai practiced a kind of Japanese rodeo in which stray dogs took the part of cattle. Naturally, the priest pointed out, this was bound to annoy Buddha. Let the shogun mend his ways. Let him begin to demonstrate a benevolent interest in the affairs of dogs, and the ladies of the Great Interior would soon each be bearing twins annually. So said Ryuko in 1687, and to Tsunayoshi the idea made sense. Almost immediately he passed the first of the Life Protecting Statutes.

In this the shogun forbade the dog rodeos and all other indignities against dogs. As for the man who actually killed a dog, that man, he ruled, had committed murder and ought to be beheaded. He meant it. A few years later his executioner did a little counting up and found that he had filled thirty barrels with the heads of those who were unable to break themselves of the practice.

Dogs who themselves attacked other dogs were the only ones exempt from this ruling. *They* were to be separated from their victims by a judicious use of cold water. A really sensitive man, Tsunayoshi suggested, would use rose-water.

Here was a promising beginning; and certainly it was far more than King William and Queen Mary of England, confronted at the same time with a similar lack of heirs, thought of attempting. As far as they were concerned, an Englishman (or an American) of 1690 could beat his dog, hitch it to a dogcart, use it to bait bulls, or even make dog soup out of it. But while the Life Protecting Statutes saved Japanese dogs from actual bodily danger, they did very little to promote canine comfort. It was still possible for a

dog even in Tokyo itself to go hungry or to have to
sleep out on the coldest night of the winter. When in
1694 the calendar came round again to the Year of
the Dog and Tsunayoshi still had no sons, he realized
that further steps were needed.

And so in the autumn of 1694, while a thousand
sheepdogs shivered in the English rain, the stray dogs
of Tokyo, to the number of fifteen thousand, were
ushered into well-heated public kennels. The shogun
had given one of his personal chamberlains, a man
named Yonekura, the task of erecting these kennels,
and it is clear that Yonekura did his work well. The
most luxurious set of kennels covered a twenty-acre
site in the fashionable suburb of Okubo. With a little
doubling up, this one kennel could accommodate
nearly ten thousand dogs in warmth and comfort. An
eight-acre kennel at Hakano housed another three
thousand. And so on.

Yonekura was raised to the peerage and permanently assigned as Grand Master of the Imperial
Japanese Kennels. On the administrative level alone,
he had the full-time assistance of four city magis-
trates, fourteen veterinarians, and sixty Imperial
police. There were those in Japan who grumbled that
the dogs might better have been assisting the police
than the other way round. Every regime has its mal-
contents.

As far as the dogs themselves were concerned,
probably the one flaw in the program was their diet. It
was ample, yes, but woefully lacking in meat. For
carried away by his own benevolence, Tsunayoshi
had presently extended the Life Protecting Statutes

to include all forms of warm-blooded life. Like the human inhabitants of the empire, the dogs of Japan thenceforth had to content themselves with a diet of rice and fish. On a typical day Lord Yonekura drew a kennel ration of twenty tons of rice, ten barrels of bean paste, and ten bales of dried sardines. Still, better a diet of fried rice and sardines in one's own warm kennel than a scrap of meat, a kick in the ribs, and a cold night in a Kentish farmyard. Or so a dog can be forgiven for feeling.

Tsunayoshi was a born optimist, and he went on practicing benevolence to dogs and hoping for sons right up to his death in 1709. When that occurred on the nineteenth of February, the Dog Star may be said to have set. His nephew and successor, Prince Iyenobu, already had a son, and was a notorious skeptic about Buddhism. Within a few weeks, 8,634 dog-beaters were hurrying home from Japanese prisons to their surprised and grateful families. Something more than twice that many state-supported dogs found themselves turned out into the world and compelled, like their ancestors, to live by their wits. Lord Yonekura found himself out of a job. A number of private citizens are reported to have found their toes inching toward newly vulnerable canine ribs. By the end of the year it was again possible in Japan to speak of a dog's life as though it were something to be avoided.

But if the pro-dog legislation of Prince Tsunayoshi failed to endure and is today largely forgotten among human beings, no doubt the dogs themselves remember. A while ago I happened to be present when an

elderly aunt of mine discovered that her Pekinese had
made a mess on the carpet.

My aunt regards this as unpardonable behavior,
and she promptly smacked the animal with a folded
newspaper. Ch'en whined and made a great show of
repentance, but under cover of this groveling I
noticed him looking at my aunt with cool, speculative
eyes. I wonder if he was recalling the days when
merely folding that newspaper would have cost the
old lady five years in jail.

Calliste Barton's Prose

Or, By the Powers,
We're Better Than I Thought

SOME PEOPLE like early American furniture. I am not one of them. What I like are early American book titles, especially two-part ones. As a matter of fact, I collect them. I can recite hundreds, and, on occasion, do.

By a two-part title I mean, of course, one with a semicolon, an *or*, and a comma bunched in the middle, forming a kind of hinge on which two independent phrases swing together. *The Blind Man's Son; or, The Poor Student Successfully Struggling to Overcome Adversity and Misfortune,* a rather eupeptic novel published by the Methodist Book Concern of New York around 1850 is a fair example of the genre. So is a somewhat better-known book of the time,

Uncle Tom's Cabin; or, Life Among the Lowly. And so, although hinged with a mere colon, is *Dental Hygeia: A Poem on Health and the Preservation of the Teeth,* With Notes by Dr. Lee, which was given to a surprised world in 1838.

Like most collections, mine has both a focus and a motive. Its focus is the fifty-year span running roughly from 1825 to 1875. During that half-century the two-part title more or less dominated American book publishing, and it is from this abundance that I chiefly collect. I do not, of course, exclude worthy specimens from other times and countries, any more than the collector of New England basket-weave chairs throws out his Chippendale. I gladly accept, inconstant spelling and all, that lively play of the 1623 London season: *The Devil's Law-Case; or, When Women Goe to Law, the Devill Is Full of Businesse.* And I not only accept, I count as one of my real prizes the title of a small book published in Hartford, Connecticut, in 1799. *The Prodigal Daughter,* it runs; *or, A strange and wonderful relation, shewing how a gentleman of great estate in Bristol, had a proud and disobedient daughter, who, because her parents would not support her in all her extravagance, bargained with the devil to poison them—How an angel informed them of her design—How she lay in a trance four days; and when she was put into the grave, she came to life again, and related the wonderful things she saw in the other world.* I've even got a few modern things, such as William Saroyan's *Razzle-Dazzle; or, The Human Ballet, Opera, and Circus,* which appeared as recently as 1942.

As for motive, mine is partly a shell collector's motive: pure delight in the intricate convolutions these titles take, wonder at their iridescent sheen. The better specimens seem to me works of art in their own right, quite independent of the books to which they are attached. I'm only sorry I can't peel them off, varnish them, and put them in cabinets.

Beyond that, the whole troubled question of advertising comes in. A modern book has a dozen means of urging itself on the reader. It can employ shiny plasticene covers or bold typography. It can give a tempting summary of itself on the inside of its jacket, or sport an appealing photograph of the author over on its rump. It can swagger about with quotations from critics on its chest, or vulgarly mention how many copies it has already sold. It is nearly certain to use bright colors and designs to catch the eye, much as certain monkeys use patches of red and blue fur.

Against all this, the nineteenth-century book depended on its title. Since it was bound soberly in brown or gray cloth [a collection of early American novels looks rather like a row of Quakers with gold teeth] it lacked anything the twentieth century would recognize as eye appeal. Having no dust jacket full of encomiums and no blurb, it was somewhat in the position of Wordsworth's Lucy: "A Maid whom there were none to praise/ And very few to love." In short, unless it happened to be by someone like Emerson or Hawthorne, it commended itself to the reader through its title or not at all.

Nineteenth-century bookmen were well aware of this fact, and hence the loving care with which they christened a new work. Hence also the keen interest with which I study the results. For example. A modern publisher, about to bring out a collection of sea stories, has his mind so full of four-color cover designs and is so taken up with deciding how many full-page ads to run that he hardly gives the title a thought. In the end he spends five minutes and calls the thing "Great Sea Stories." The firm of Stringer and Townsend, confronted with the same problem in 1854, sucked their pencils rather longer. *Their* anthology was called *"Swell Life at Sea; or, Fun, Frigates, and Yachting; a Collection of Nautical Yarns."* Consider what they worked in. Here is first of all a distinctive name for the book; secondly, implied praise of it ("swell" and "fun"); thirdly, a kind of visual image for it (a sea-swell with dozens of frigates and yachts gently bobbing up and down); and fourthly, a suggestion that the authors know their stuff. (These are not mere lubberly stories, but "nautical yarns.") They don't make titles like that any more.

Another example. The sort of book that in our time is called by some cryptic phrase like "Who's Who," and given crimson covers, had once a fine appellation and a brown binding. There was one in that same year of 1854 called *You Have Heard of Them; being Sketches of Statesmen and Politicians, Painters, Instrumentalists and Vocalists, Authors and Authoresses.* This I find in every way more satisfactory. It may be that our modern book couldn't adopt the old name entirely, because one so often *hasn't* heard of the people in it, but it might at least have preserved the distinction between statesmen and politicians.

And note the fine periphrastic ring of "instrumentalists and vocalists." As description of contents, the one word "musicians" would have covered the ground and taken in composers, as well—just as "authors" really includes both sexes. Here is obviously the nineteenth-century equivalent of scarlet boards and a half-page ad in the Chicago *Tribune*.

One can produce a similar noble ancestor for almost every sort of book now being produced. In place of the blunt *World Almanac,* the mid-nineteenth century had *Inquire Within; or, Over Three Thousand Seven Hundred Facts Worth Knowing.* In place of the beats, it had *Gentleman Jack; or, Life on the Road,* published anonymously in 1861. Rather than the official guidebooks that proliferate now, it had joyful volumes like the one Eliza Farnham wrote in 1856: *California, In-Doors and Out; or, How We Farm, Mine, and Live Generally in the Golden State.* Yes, and if some Easterner, carried away by that matchless title, headed West to seek his fortune, his wife back in Vermont simply wrote off to Philadelphia for a copy of *Lonely Hours: A Text-Book of Knitting.*

Even nineteenth-century medical books felt the call to two-part titles. Dr. Davis's *Acute Hydrocephalus; or, Water in the Head,* 1840, is readily matched by Dr. Bowditch's *The Young Stethoscopist; or, The Student's Guide to Auscultation,* 1846, not to mention Dr. Harrison's *The Dublin Dissector; or, Manual of Anatomy,* which appeared in a pirate edition in Washington, D.C., in 1835. One of my particular favorites belongs in none of these categories but is a humbler book, a handyman's manual, published in New York in 1864. I mean the now-forgotten *How to Do It; or, Directions for Knowing and Doing Everything Needful*. What book now has such a sweep to its title? None. If a man wanted to match it, he'd have to go back in the other direction, perhaps to 1857, when Lieutenant A. W. Habersham of the United States Navy published a short book of travels. *My Last Cruise,* he called it; *Being an Account of Visits to the Malay and Loo-Choo Islands, the Coasts of China, Formosa, Japan, Kamschatka, Siberia, and the Mouth of the Amoor River*. A book like that doesn't even need end papers; its map is right there in the title.

And yet, curious and convoluted as many of these are, they are by no means the plums of my collection. There's another kind of two-part name that I've hardly mentioned. Most of the ones I've been talking about are essentially newspaper titles: The second part amplifies the first in the same way that a subhead does a headline. They are good, intricate nomenclature—far richer and stranger than anything publishers think of today, to be sure—but essentially factual. Their modest aim was to sell nineteenth-century reference books. When it came to nineteenth-century fiction, a different principle was employed. Instead of the semicolon, *or,* and comma being a hinge on which the two parts of the title swung together, it became a reef on which they veered apart. The aim was not to amplify but to mystify, not to shout wares like a Yankee huckster but to offer tantalizing glimpses like a Charleston coquette. So effectively do some of the titles do this that a true connoisseur of double-titled nineteenth-century novels seldom reads them, even if he can find copies, for fear that the actual events of the novel will interfere with the delicious fancies conjured up by the name.

Take my own dealings with an 1856 novel called *Married, Not Mated; or, How They Lived at Woodside and Throckmorton Hall*. I've never read it, nor seen a copy. I know nothing about Alice Cary, who wrote it, and don't want to. My mind is fully occupied with that title, which has for me about two hundred possibilities. Who, for example, are "they"? One young couple with two houses? Two couples, one pair at Woodside Cottage and the other in the great plantation house known as Throckmorton Hall? I can't tell. And what's this about being married but not mated? Is Miss Cary contrasting a true union for romantic love to some squalid match for money? Or does she mean a Platonic marriage? Maybe two? Yes, I think perhaps two Platonic marriages. I seem to see two sisters, young, beautiful, orphaned. Their cruel guardian has forcibly engaged them, one to a merchant's son in the little town of Woodside, the other to the young squire of Throckmorton Hall. Late the night before their wedding, the two girls take a vow—

But at this point I always stop. I feel that I've solved Miss Cary's plot, and now I am anxious to get on to other books. There was one published in 1858 that I always like to get on to. It contains in the simple word "in" one of the most ambiguous prepositions in the history of American publishing. *Colum-*

bia, the Beautiful Blonde; or, Life in the Fifth Avenue, New York, the book is entitled, and much depends on how you see life "in" an avenue, whether you envision it as taking place in the houses alongside or right there on the cobblestones. I've already made up *my* mind. I think Columbia is a peddler's daughter who lives in her father's pushcart on the west side of Fifth, probably around Twenty-second Street. I can see the opening scene vividly. It's about quarter to eight on a bright spring morning. Columbia's father is seated by the pushcart, carefully uncrating a shipment of Venetian beads, while Columbia herself, clad in a pretty dressing gown, is just mincing across the Avenue to go and wash her face at the old watering trough in Madison Square. At that instant who should come cantering up, his horse half mad with thirst, but—

Again, this is where I always stop. I could readily give that young horseman a name and a fine old New York fortune and a mother who disapproves of peddlers, but that would be descending into factualism. I'd much rather get on to *Richard Edney and the Governor's Family: A Rus-Urban Tale, Simple and Popular, Yet Cultured and Noble, of Morals, Sentiment, and Life, Practically Treated and Pleasantly Illustrated, Containing, Also, Hints on Being Good and Doing Good.* That was a Boston novel, as the second part of its title suggests, and sometimes I've been tempted actually to read it. Even in an age which routinely produced books entitled things like *Ways of Life, Showing the Right Way and the Wrong Way* and *Kenneth Forbes; or, Fourteen Ways of Studying the Bible,* it seems to offer unusual opportunities for self-improvement. But it also offers rather fine speculation, and that I have been unwilling to give up. My vision of the book is a particularly strong one. I think the rus- part of this rus-urban tale is the Governor himself: a simple, popular and, alas, totally illiterate politician from up-country. Richard Edney I see as the urban part, the cultured and noble Bostonian whom the new Governor engages to read his mail for him. As for the Governor's family, well, they're full of morals, sentiment, and life. Country life. The more cultured and noble Edney is, the more he will be drawn by the pathos of that sentimental middle-aged woman and her two lively but clodhopping daughters making fools of themselves in Boston society. In particular he will blush at the mother's shameless attempts to get Brahmin husbands for her girls. He can't help feeling they should stick to the farm boys they knew back home. Litterateur that he is, I think he will read to them from a popular novel of the time which turns on this very problem, the famous *John; or, Is a Cousin in the Hand worth two Counts in the Bush?* He will not, of course, convince them, and in the end Edney is going to have to marry one of those girls himself.

There was a time when I could almost have envied him. Clodhoppers those girls may be, but they are early nineteenth-century clodhoppers. An age which produced the book in which they appear, I would have argued, has so much more vitality than our own as to be worth living in at any price. But I can argue that way no longer. As I've implied, I usually don't read double-titled books, I just talk about them. Last winter I made the mistake of talking once too often about my favorite of the whole species: Dr. Ariel Ivers Cummings' 1847 novel *The Factory Girl; or, Gardez la Coeur*. The result is that this spring one of my uncles ran across a copy in a secondhand bookstore in Maine and promptly sent it to me. Not content with admiring its quiet brown cover and chaste typography, I read it. A whole universe has tumbled.

For years my greatest delight has been to invent plots for *The Factory Girl*. Since I knew the book was published in Lowell, Massachusetts, I have always used the same background, namely the great nineteenth-century spinning mills there. But the girl herself varied from week to week. Sometimes, excited by that delectable caution, *Gardez la Coeur* (which, please note, is in the second-person plural: we were *all* to guard our hearts), I made her a French emigré, the daughter perhaps of a Napoleonic general, now here in plain old Massachusetts, working at the mill and undoing the emotions of every young Cabot or Lowell who rode out from Boston to inspect his investments. Sometimes I made her a gray-eyed beauty from Quebec, speaking with an adorable French-Canadian accent, handling the spindles with flying fingers, and destroying the serenity of every farmer's son from Chelmsford to Tyngsboro. Sometimes I saw her an emancipated American girl, brisk and delicious of speech, full of notions about women's rights, scornfully refusing offers of marriage from foreman after foreman at the mills. In any case, what I imagined the novel to be was a kind of Shaw comedy before Shaw, a verbal pyrotechnic of the eighteen forties, the kind of book you're so busy hugging yourself with delight over that you can hardly spare a hand to turn the pages. What I got was—well, different. But let Dr. Cummings speak for himself. This is how his book opens:

Never, perhaps, did the "Manchester of America" [Lowell, he means], though renowned for the moral and intellectual worth of its inhabitants, and especially its Female Operatives, bear within its limits a nobler, more pure, and worthy soul than that which caused the heart of CALLISTE BARTON to beat, in her humble sphere. In saying this, it is no disparagement to anyone, as we trust the following pages will show.

And now, courteous reader, we invite you to follow us, if you please, through a series of scenes which, though delineated in a familiar style, and without the magic graces of—

No, the rest of this paragraph is intolerable. My eye refuses to follow it. Let me start again with the next paragraph.

It was a beautiful evening in mid-summer, in the year 18__. The brilliant constellations had taken their seats in the blue vault of heaven, and every star seemed to twinkle with joy, and to emit its rays like the benign influence of the virtuous mind upon surrounding objects. The zephyrs—

I'm sorry, I can't go on. What those zephyrs are doing is wafting a load of fragrance across a pellucid stream, and they are an unconscionably long time

about it. One hears the last of them only to encounter
Dame Nature herself, holding a magic wand in her
hand, with which she has just finished animating the
countryside. I'll make a third start with the paragraph that follows.

On such an evening as this, at a short distance from a
small, yet beautiful village of the "Granite State" [New
Hampshire, we call it now], upon the banks of a stream
tributary to the noble river [the Connecticut] that washes
the western boundary of that State, might have been seen,
apparently in deep and interesting, if not anxious conversation, a lady and gentleman, whose appearance would
particularly have engaged your attention. They were both
young, and the lady at least was peculiarly beautiful and
lovely.
"When shall you return, Calliste?" inquired the gentleman. "That is uncertain," was the reply. "We shall miss
you," continued the first speaker, "but I hope we shall
hear from you often." "Most certainly I shall write," she
replied. But we have traced their conversation far enough
to open to the minds of our readers the characters which
we have introduced—and as the companion of Calliste, at
the present time, permit us to introduce MARCUS HART-
WELL, of whom the reader will hear more as we proceed.
Suffice it to say, that he was a *very dear friend* of Calliste,
and that they were about to part for a season.

This is something more like. At least through the
rumble and crash of old-fashioned oratory we're
beginning to hear human voices. But if anyone sup-
poses that the dialogue will continue, that we're going
to get another syllable from the lips of Calliste and
Marcus before she starts down to Lowell and her

new job at the factory, he has a lot to learn about early nineteenth-century fiction. Oh, the two of them keep on talking—"Long did they converse, seated upon the moss-covered bank, beneath the shade of a majestic elm [mind you, it's after dark], whose towering trunk had bid defiance to the storms of many a rolling year, ere those beneath its boughs had commenced the journey of life"—it's just not reported. In fact, the next human voices become audible six chapters later, nearly a year after Calliste has reached Lowell and started her career as a factory girl. And these voices make it clear, I regret to say, that the warning about guarding *la coeur* applies to Calliste herself, rather than to the young men of the vicinity.

In the intervening five chapters, Calliste has written a letter to Marcus and thought a good deal about her brother Edwin, whom she is working to put through college. As to what she's up to in Lowell, we hear nothing about the spinning mills, but only that she and another factory girl named Louisa Elliot are living in a boardinghouse, from which they venture out to divine service each Sunday. It is this that leads to the mischief. Chapter Seven begins thus:

"Who were those two young ladies that I pointed out to you at church to-day?" inquired Cassius Wilson [only favorable characters are introduced with capitals], a spring of southern chivalry, of Alfred Boyden, as they sipped their wine in the private room of the latter, in a splendid mansion on _____ street.

"O, they were only factory girls," replied the latter,

with a toss of his head and a grin of contempt on his countenance.

"*Factory girls,* did you say? Had you said birds of paradise, or angels, you would not so much have astonished me. Why, if I am any judge of beauty, I never saw a nymph nearer the perfection of the *Venus de Medicis,* than were one of them. . . . By the way, are you acquainted with them, Alfred?"

"Acquainted with *factory girls!* What do you ask me such a question for? Do you suppose that I would disgrace my character by associating with that class? Not I, unless it were for a little fun, or a _____ of a conquest. . . ."

"But," continued Cassius, "do you know where they reside, and what they bear for names? Come now, be honest and tell me, for at least one of them is a *rara avis* —beautiful—and worth a short acquaintance, by the powers!"

"Yes," replied Alfred, "I know them, and where they reside, but they are as shy as the very _____, and one of them is most insuperable and unapproachable minx that you ever did see, and by the way, they live with a cursed widow, who is as pious as you please, and keeps them tied to her apron strings—though Ned Rawson and I served her a _____ of a trick once, and came nigh enjoying a *tête à tête* with the girls, but were put off by a singular and _____ unfortunate circumstance, which I will not now relate."

"Good on your head, by _____!" exclaimed Cassius, "the game is still fresh, and I swear we will become further acquainted with these same *factory girls,* and if we fail, there are enough more fine noble fowls for our picking!"

. . . Thus they laid their plans for the accomplishment of their hellish purposes. Here we pause to notice briefly their circumstances, as the reader will at once recognize their character.

This reader, at least, did recognize their character, and very pleased I was with it. I had been counting on a Shavian comedy, with Calliste Barton breaking hearts left and right, but a hellish plot against her own has its points, too. If I can't get comedy, I'll settle for melodrama; and the presence of Cassius Wilson seemed to guarantee a good one. I liked his phrase about the "fine noble fowls" especially. It has just the touch of cold-bloodedness that one demands of a serious-minded villain. I found myself waiting eagerly to see how the young hellion would mount his assault.

It was no long wait, either. The very next Wednesday after that fateful church service, Calliste and Louisa sallied out after work to the Lowell Lyceum, to hear a lecture. Many hundreds of other factory girls also sallied out, and in fact the whole town was there, villains included. In those days villains still took an interest in culture. I don't pretend they took an interest only in that: ogling factory girls before the lecture began was clearly a leading diversion at the Lowell Lyceum. Nor was it all covert. When the beautiful Calliste and the fair Louisa arrived, there was a quite noticeable ripple and stir all along Villains' Row. Alfred Boyden and Cassius Wilson went so far as to swivel their heads around and stare openly. It was the kind of stare few men are capable of now.

As the panther, less to be dreaded than such characters, eyes his prey with apparent delight, ere he destroys it, so did the demon spirits in the garb, and bearing the name of *gentlemen*, look upon their intended victims. And still the objects were unconscious of the proposed infernal agency! Beautiful, guileless and lovely beings, they knew not their danger!

Naturally after this kind of look I expect something fairly pantherine to occur. Whether Alfred and Cassius mean to use guile or force, I can't tell, but I look for the stroke to be a bold one. Perhaps they will buy up the mortgage on Calliste's father's farm. No, too slow. I think maybe they'll kidnap the girls this very night. Already I can fancy a midnight wine-party at the splendid mansion on —————— Street. Drugged wine. But, hush, here comes the critical moment.

The exercises of the evening were closed, and the crowd began to disperse. A drizzling shower of rain had commenced falling, and Cassius and Alfred waited at a post nigh the doors, ready for their expedition; but what was their surprise and mortification to find themselves *nonplussed* [that's the second time in a row for Alfred] by a flat refusal of their company from Calliste and Louisa, their intended victims!

And that, I am sorry to say, is the end of that. In what I can't help thinking is a most un-pantherlike fashion, Alfred and Cassius take no for an answer and plod off through the rain. They buy no mortgage, make no attempt to see the girls again, and in fact vanish out of the novel entirely with the passage I have just quoted. I wouldn't be surprised to hear of them both, five years hence, as missionaries to the Loo-Choo Islands.

As for the book, it has eleven of its twenty chapters still to go, and practically nothing to fill them except bad writing. Calliste's heart hasn't a single peril left to guard itself against, not so much as an amorous glance from a fellow worker during lunch hour at the mill. Nothing remains but for her to marry the faithful Marcus Hartwell, which she does at the end of the book, and to find a husband for Louisa, which she does in the intervening ten chapters.

What happens, briefly, is that about four years after that evening at the Lyceum, Calliste invites Louisa up to New Hampshire for a visit. Within a week of their arrival, brother Edwin turns up. He has now graduated first in his class at ———— College and finished his studies at ———— Divinity School, and is just about to be ordained. Unlike Alfred and Cassius, down in Lowell, he seems utterly placid in the presence of beautiful factory girls. It's a Saturday night when he gets home, and by way of celebration he goes straight off to bed. The next morning he takes the two lovely creatures to church with him. And then?

The services of the forenoon were completed, and the exercises of the Sabbath School gained the attention of Calliste and her friend, while Edwin, by request of the Pastor, retired to the parsonage.

A panther, observing the scene, would bite off his claws in sheer disgust.

And yet, there is method in this. As Edwin well knows, a factory girl doesn't want to be stared at in public, she wants tender glances reserved for her private moments. Consequently, he bides his time until late one evening, when everybody in the small but beautiful village is asleep—or, as Dr. Cummings expresses it, until "Morpheus had locked the human family, at least those in this hemisphere, in her embrace." He then leads the willing Louisa into the parlor and pops her into his. And as far as events go, the novel is over, along with my illusions about early nineteenth-century writing.

It is too late for me to stop collecting double titles. I don't even promise to quit weaving fantasies around them, though I shall not again weave with the old abandon. But it will, I think, be a long time before I pick up some forgotten old novel, no matter how fascinating its title or seemly its binding, and sit down for a good read. I'll go further. If some day, traveling in Greece, I come on the lost poems of Sappho in a cave, or the missing comedies of Sophocles under the Temple of Apollo, I shall take out my matches, and for the honor of the past I shall quietly and reverently burn every scrap of manuscript in sight.

Wake me up for the hoedown

DOWN IN VIRGINIA, where I received part of
my education at an obscure boarding school far out
in the country and high up in the mountains— Let me
start over. Down and out and up in Virginia, when I
was in the second form at school, we used to study
English grammar. Our teacher had been with the
Dock Street Theatre in Charleston for a couple of
years, before the lack of acting ability from which he
so conspicuously suffered led him to pedagogy, and
he brought his theatrical bias with him. I can remember being one of the Nouns in a classroom play he
wrote for us, in which the grammatis personae, as
he insisted on calling them, consisted entirely of parts
of speech. I also remember hating it, because I
thought the Adverbs had all the good lines.

The rather odd view of grammar I then acquired has stayed with me, however, and even now the word "verb" conjures up for me a twelve-year-old boy in a track suit (to signalize action), while a "noun" means myself at the same age, in an Eton collar (I was a Proper Noun), being harried by several Adjectives. The Adverbs, in case you're interested, got to carry whips, with which they could menace, though not actually strike, the shivering Verbs. Never was I an Adverb. Later, when we played punctuation, it was three times my fate to be the upper half of a Semicolon.

All of this, as I say, has given me a permanently buskined view of the English language, and recently, when I came to realize a disturbing truth about those little words one uses with nouns and verbs (*I* call them Prepositions), I found I could express it only in dramatic form. This I have done in the following ten scenes. The human personae who figure in these scenes are too many to be listed or described, and in any event all that matter here are the Prepositions. They matter terribly. Up and Down are my heroes; In and Out play minor supporting roles.

Gillian Barker, who was a nervous woman, turned to her husband. "For heaven's sake, slow up, Arthur," she said. "You know how I hate it when you speed on these curvy roads. It's bad for my heart."

Eighteen seconds later, she turned to her husband again. "Arthur," she repeated, "I *asked* you to slow down."

Mr. Barker permitted a faint smile to crease his

lips. "No, hon," he said. "You asked me to slow up."

"Miss! Miss!" Archibald Effinger called to the clerk. "Will you take this money, please? I want to pay up my down payment."

"Pay down at the other end," the girl said irritably. "It's the window marked 'Cashier.'"

When Effinger arrived at the window, however, the money he had brought proved to be insufficient. His down payment had been upped.

Frank Simonecka and Fred Moore, who had worked in the same textile mill in Massachusetts for twelve years, until the company folded up (i.e., closed down), walked past the silent plant. "They've really shut the place up," remarked Moore. "Look, they've even got the windows boarded. You think we'll ever work there again?"

"Nah," answered Frank, who expected the worst from life. "Once a New England plant shuts down, that's the end. This place is closed up for good."

Postscript: A few weeks later, the two men set out in opposite directions—Moore down to New York, and Simonecka down to Maine—and soon both had better jobs than ever before in their lives.

Mrs. Henry Blute eyed her husband contemptuously as he came down to breakfast. He was not a man who came up to her specifications. "Well," she demanded, "what are *you* all dressed up for? Aren't you going in to the office?"

"Sure I am," said Mr. Blute. "That's why I got my

good suit on. I told you last week, it's the annual sales meeting. What's the matter? You want me to get another dressing down like I did two years ago?"

"Listen, wise guy, shut up," Big Bill Conroy growled, fingering his shoulder holster.

"You heard him," chimed in Big Bill's sidekick, Armand Higgins. "Pipe down."

The stranger continued to argue.

"Will you knock it off?" Conroy shouted, beside himself with fury.

"Yeah, cut it out!" Armand snarled.

Their anger frightened a nursemaid who was sitting on a nearby park bench with her two charges. "Hush up, babies," she said to the children. She meant that she wanted them to keep their voices down.

Mrs. Peter Ix poured two fresh cups of coffee. "First off, he had to come down with this terrible cold," she said to her friend Helen Beals. "He's been laid up for a week, and him on his vacation, too." By "him" she meant her husband's younger brother. "But what really broke him up was that hussy's going off to Florida anyway."

"I'm not surprised," said Mrs. Beals. "If you ask me, he's never been the same since he had the breakdown."

"Of course we're going Dutch, Mother," said young Mrs. Heldon, settling comfortably down in her theater seat. "We'll settle up afterwards. This is one time

I can afford it. Remember, I told you there was this big shake-up in Ted's company and he was going to get a promotion? Well, he really shook them down. I bet he's making as much as Dad does."

"I hear Conroy's been tumbled by the new gang," Inspector Ward remarked to the police commissioner. "That must have been some fight."

The police commissioner nodded. "So I hear," he said. "And quite a comedown for Conroy. I understand *he's* paying protection to *them* now. Yes, sir, Big Bill has really had his comeuppance."

"Well, well, we *are* looking up," Dr. Prink said, somewhat inaccurately, as he was at that moment looking down Gillian Barker's throat. He straightened, and signaled his nurse. "Would you mind if I wrote down a few notes, Mrs. Barker? It's such an unusual case I might just write it up."

"Capital!" exclaimed Sir Jenkins Watley, the famous archeologist. "If that clay stratum means anything, I believe we've hit the spot on the first go. Have the men work down steadily, Bevan, and I think we'll be in the burial chamber before tea."

"Is that wise, sir?" Bevan Coggeshell asked. "I mean, these natives have never done any real digging before. Don't you think we should have them work up to the burial chamber gradually?"

"Oh, work it out any way you like, Bevan—you're the field chief," Sir Jenkins said heavily. "I'm off to have a look round. Want to work off a bit of this lunch." Work away, you young puppy, he thought, and see where it gets you.

Bevan felt disappointed. The old explorer didn't use to give up so easily. Pity, he said to himself—I had a few more good digs to work in.

Sir Jenkins strode off down the narrow ridge. As he walked, he began working over in his mind his next report to the trustees. He chuckled at the thought of all the damaging details he could work in. Bevan might never get an archeological job again. Work up to a tomb, will you, he thought. We'll see who gets worked down into one. Thoroughly worked up, he forgot to look where he was going and walked straight off a cliff where the path turned. That same day two jackals had him worked down to the bone.

A health to England, every guest

"NORMALLY HER FATHER would do it," Trevor said, putting his hand on my shoulder, "but the poor fellow stammers."

"Annie's father? What would he normally do?" I asked in my usual impetuous way. Trevor was, however, in mid-peroration and unable to stop.

"Her Uncle Derrick could do it," he continued, "but I think it's fair to say that Uncle Derrick is the most consistently boring conversationalist in the North Riding. Her cousin Ted could do it—in fact, we had counted on him to—but his firm is sending him on a sudden business trip to Denmark. So Annie said why not ask you."

"Ask me *what*, Trev?"

"Why, to propose the toast to her at our reception. Didn't I say that? I realize four days is short notice, but we'd both be frightfully pleased if you would. And you know Annie, she likes to be different."

I did know Annie—she was Trevor's fiancée, a bright-haired, rosy-cheeked girl from the top of York-shire—but of English weddings I was entirely igno-rant. I was only an overseas student in his first year of graduate work at Cambridge University, a naive and trusting scholar. In my innocence I thought Trevor meant he wanted me to say a few words over a glass of champagne, as we sometimes do at wed-dings at home. I was flattered to be asked.

"Well, gosh, Trev," I said. "Sure. If her family really won't mind me butting in, I'll be glad to say a good word for Annie."

"Bless you," said Trevor. "That's one problem solved. Now I've got to pop round and see the chap-lain. It's a bit of a bind, this getting married in Cam-bridge."

The next afternoon I discovered what he meant. I was taking tea with an elegant Londoner named Godfrey Forbes-Bentinck who lived in the same court of our six-hundred-year-old college as Trevor and I.

"I hear your friend Chubb is getting married in the college chapel and that we're all asked," Godfrey said, fitting a couple of scones on his silver toasting forks and propping them in front of the fire. "Are you going?"

"Going? I'm practically the star attraction."

"Why do you always assume that no one has ever seen an American before?" Godfrey said irritably.

"You people stopped being novelties here around 1850. You weren't *interesting* novelties even then."

"Be yourself, Godfrey," I said. "I only meant that Trevor's asked me to give a toast to Annie at the reception."

Godfrey stared at me in frank surprise. "You're giving the bride's health? What's the matter with her father?"

"He stammers."

"No uncles?"

"Yes, but it happens that Trevor asked me."

"He must be off his rocker. Fancy asking *you*."

"Gee, Godfrey, thanks a bunch."

"Well, I mean it," he said, passing me my tea. "He's mad to have asked you, and you're madder to have accepted. After all, how well do you know this girl that Chubb is marrying?"

"We aren't friends from childhood, obviously. I've had dinner with her and Trev a couple of times, and I took her punting once while Trev was seeing his supervisor, and I guess I saw her in London once. But so what?"

"Then how are you going to know what to say?"

I grinned. "I gotta ready wit."

Godfrey grinned. "I take it you also have a good script writer."

"Hunh?"

Godfrey took the scones, now somewhat scorched, off the forks and began to butter them. "I believe you really don't have these abominations in the States."

"We are accustomed to get married, if that's what you mean."

"I mean toasts. Wedding toasts are the blight of England. The whole ritual of getting married is. I may very well remain celibate on account of it."

"Why, Godfrey, you sensitive thing."

"You'll wish Chubb had been half as sensitive, before you're done," Godfrey said warningly. "Let me tell you what an English wedding reception is like. I mean, of course, a lower middle-class affair like Chubb's."

"I thought your father was in trade himself."

"How any mention of class embarrasses Americans. Do you want to hear or not?"

"I might as well say yes. You're obviously going to tell me anyway."

"You're right," said Godfrey. "I am. Only it's all so bloody I hardly know where to begin. I think I'll skip the first hour, which, if I know the lower middle class, you'll spend drinking bad sherry out of claret glasses. I'll even spare you the first piece of ritual, namely the reading of the telegrams, the three humorous ones, all in execrable taste, from school friends of the groom, the seventeen treacly ones, in even worse taste, from those relatives on both sides whom a generous fate has spared one the actual presence of. In fact, I think I'll begin with the toasts, which are normally the next event after the telegrams. You know when they're coming by a ten-minute silence that suddenly falls.

"When no one can stand it any longer, the best man makes a sign to a designated relative of the groom's, usually whichever of his aunts has the biggest bosom. She advances to one end of the room, clutching a sheaf of notes, and proceeds to make a formal speech—an oration, actually—covering every incident in the groom's life from his birth on. He's her favorite nephew, she says. They always knew he'd turn out well, she says. They're proud of him now, she adds, and her voice trembles. She collapses into a chair and begins to snivel. The bride's father, who has been waiting impatiently for this to happen, now springs up.

"*He* doesn't have any notes; he doesn't need them. He's got his speech by heart. So, in fact, does his wife, who composed it, making sure that it would run at least five minutes longer than the groom's aunt's. He is nothing if not complete. He tells you how his Gillian won a Healthy Baby award from the County Council at the age of seven months, and had all her teeth at two. Then he tells you what a dear little nipper she was at three and a half, with her long blond ringlets and her chubby smile, and how everyone said she would grow up to be a real heartbreaker and sure enough she did. Then—"

"Oh, really, Godfrey. Has no one ever told you about traditional British understatement?"

"I'm using it. I swear. And I'm not done, either. Let me finish. He implies that fine and clean and decent as his new son-in-law is, Gillian could have made a considerably better match, had she chosen to. The groom's mother makes strangling noises. He hurries on to tell what a good cook Gillian is, and how clever around the house. In extreme cases he may even hint with a kind of pious leer at the connubial bliss in store for the fortunate young man. Finally, gasping with emotion, he tells you that now Gillian is leaving home, life is over for him. He brushes away a manly tear. His wife goes into spastic fit. The other women present begin to keen. It is sickening beyond belief."

"Go on. Then what happens," I said bravely.

"Why, if you've survived all that, you're in the clear," Godfrey said, a touch of annoyance in his tone that I should still be able to ask. "All who can stomach the sherry proceed to get drunk, and it is sometimes even rather pleasant. But you won't survive."

In this prediction Godfrey was mistaken. We Americans are fighters. Practically abandoning my dissertation, I spent the three days that remained to me in getting up my toast. I talked to everyone I could find who had given one. Annie had arrived in Cambridge; and, prying her loose from a pile of thank-you letters (she was writing them in advance and post-dating them), I put her through an interview that would have done credit to Dr. Krafft-Ebing. I even practiced choking up.

And when the nuptial day arrived I was ready. During the actual service, a small one in our tiny medieval chapel, I was probably more nervous than Annie or Trev, but I was ready. I had a heightened version of Annie's life history memorized, and I delivered it movingly, some hour and a half after we arrived at the local restaurant where the reception was being held. It wasn't easy to be moving, after the lurid account of Trevor we had just had, but I managed. Even Trevor's two aunts laughed at my jokes, and at the end the elder of them, the one who was a retired Liverpool policewoman, was weeping freely. My sinuous references to Annie's probable good qualities as a wife caused Annie herself to redden with pleasure, and the other four graduate students present to eye her with a new interest.

My one regret was that Godfrey wasn't there to hear me, he and the Hon. Brian Lascelles, the other elegant research student in College, having gone off on Brian's motor scooter for an upper-class weekend. "Have a jolly day with the trogs," Godfrey called to me as they left, looking rather troggish himself in crash helmet and goggles, as of course Brian did, too. "Trog" is short for troglodyte, or cave dweller, and in my day at Cambridge it was the fashionable term for a member of the proletariat (or prole). In America, I think, the equivalent word is yokel, except at Dartmouth College, where it's emmet.

Trevor was almost embarrassingly grateful. The minute I'd finished speaking, he came over, holding Annie with one hand and a bottle of the terrible sherry which the restaurant had provided in the other. "Your toast was a smasher," he assured me not less than four times. "You couldn't have done better" —and here he looked the way I imagine the Queen does when she's about to bestow a knighthood—"if you'd been English yourself. Even Aunt Phyllis said so." Aunt Phyllis had delivered *his* eulogium. He paused and shot an imploring glance at Annie.

"Oh, Trevor, you ask him," she said.

Trevor looked me bravely in the eye. "Here's the thing of it," he said. "It's four o'clock. We've done our duty by the dear old fam and all, and we do rather want to get away. But we've the problem of what to do with Annie's parents."

He hesitated again, and Annie took firmly over. "Mum and Dad have to get back to Yorkshire tonight," she said. "They've never been in the south of England before, and they're feeling a bit edgy-like. They don't even know how to get to the station."

This was obviously my cue. "Would you like me to take them?" I asked.

Trevor's face lit up. "I say, would you? Lord, it would help us. Are you sure it wouldn't be a bother?"

"Trev thinks we've asked you too much already," Annie broke in, "but you're our only close friend with a car. Besides, what I told him is, Americans *like* driving people about. I used to know some of your Air Force fellows in York, and they thought nothing of driving twenty miles to take a girl to dinner, driving twenty miles on to a dance, and then driving her forty miles home again after."

"We're a motorized people," I agreed. "Shall I go on and take them now?"

"Soon," said Annie, slipping the sherry bottle out of Trevor's hand and putting it on a table. "We're just going to change, we won't be ten minutes, and then we'll be back to say good-by. We've one last favor. Could you sort of look after Mum and Dad meanwhile? Then you could drop them off at the station directly we leave. We'd be ever so grateful."

It would have been the act of a trog to refuse now.

Naturally Annie and Trev spent rather more than ten minutes changing. Even I had known they would.

What I hadn't expected was the blighting effect
their absence would have. I was looking for the pleasant drunken part that Godfrey had mentioned. It
failed to materialize. The minute the newlyweds left,
we all sprang away from the refreshments. Huddled
across the room, we began a kind of antiphonal chant
about the weather. How nice for Trevor and Annie,
half of us remarked to the other half, that it is not
raining. Not every young couple is so lucky, the
other half replied. Someone remembered a wedding
in 1934 during which hail fell. And then the four
other research students from College left in a group,
taking Trevor's good-looking cousin Joan and Annie's
friend Hilary Thompson with them. The two chem-
ists from Trevor's lab left immediately after. The one
of them who had been best man and read the telegrams (a mere eight) at least had the grace to apolo-
gize as he left.

"Tell Trev we waited forty minutes," he said. "And
tell him I want him and Annie to come round for a
drink the minute they get back next week. But I simply must look in at the lab before it closes." He hurried off.

With his departure the company was thinned out
to a kind of hard core, consisting of Trevor's parents
and his two aunts and uncle-in-law, Annie's parents
and her twelve-year-old brother, and me. Oh, yes,
there was also Mrs. Ashford, the wife of Trevor's
supervisor at the chem labs, who had come alone.
(Her husband, one of the great scientists of Cambridge, invariably accepted invitations, and invariably neglected to turn up. *Her* practice was to accept,

turn up, and then stay practically forever, supposedly because she could never think of any plausible excuse for leaving.) She was a handsome woman about forty.

Trevor's parents and uncle-in-law and aunts were worried about time. The five of them had come up from Eastbourne, Sussex, where they all lived, in a hired car. They were anxious to get started back before dark. So, apparently, was their driver. Looking out the windows of our upstairs banqueting room, you could see his big Humber parked below on King's Parade and him stalking around polishing it with little impatient swipes.

"Where can those two lovebirds be?" asked Trevor's Aunt Phyllis, looking at the enameled watch which dangled down her impressive front on a ribbon. "We shan't be home until after nine o'clock."

Annie's mother, near whom I was hovering, in the hope that presently one of us would lapse into conversation, glanced at her own watch but said nothing. Obviously she didn't intend to expose her Yorkshire accent to possible ridicule from these dapper Sussex people. She and her husband and son were sitting in three stiff banquet chairs with their hands folded in their laps. Mrs. Ashford was looking out the window in a distraught way.

I continued to hope for conversational inspiration, but none came, and the next sound to break the silence was the voice of Trevor's father. He had taken out his watch to check Aunt Phyllis's computations, and he had found them unsound. "It'll be more like

a half past nine before we get there," he said authori-
tatively.

If there was any social capital to be made out of
this remark, it occurred to none of us. My own mind
was torn between a desire to have a glass of sherry
and another piece of wedding cake—it was one of
those vast cakes, an inch thick with marzipan, which
chiefly redeem the gastronomics of a people whose
favorite vegetable is the Brussels sprout—and a feeling that any return to the food table would be regarded by the others present as frivolous, or even
wicked. It was left to Mrs. Ashford to try to reassert
a carnival air. With a decisive gesture she opened the
window in front of which she'd been standing.
Thrusting her head out, she took a sort of survey of
what was to be seen, being careful to ignore the
hired car from Eastbourne and its driver, who had
got hold of a pocket gauge and was checking the
pressure in his tires.

"If you look a bit over here to the right," Mrs.
Ashford said, pulling her head back in and raising
her voice, "you can get rather a fine view of King's
College Chapel. It was completed in 1515 and is perhaps the finest example of late Gothic church architecture in England. Further down you can just make
out the Senate House and the beautiful old tower of
St. John's."

She paused expectantly, and moved by an obscure
impulse I went dutifully over and peered out at the
familiar bulk of King's. No one else budged. "It will
be quite ten o'clock," Aunt Phyllis said dolefully behind me.

Her husband snorted. "You forget that we've Muriel to take down to the Lewes Road after we get there. Four miles each way. And not a sign of Trevor. We may not get off for another half-hour. Mark my words, we shall be damn lucky to be home before eleven."

This gloomy prediction clearly shook them all. "Perhaps we shouldn't wait," Aunt Muriel said in a depressed but tentative way. "I'm sure Trevor wouldn't want us to."

"Wait? Of course we're going to wait," Trevor's father snapped, looking miserable. "I'm surprised at you, Muriel. Thinking of yourself at a time like this."

Aunt Muriel looked so guilty, so hangdog, even, at this accusation of the sin of personality that apparently her sister's heart was moved. At any rate, Aunt Phyllis, once a Liverpool policewoman and long since an Eastbourne matron, came thundering to the rescue.

"And what about Mr. Clapford?" she demanded. "Are we to keep *him* waiting forever? Fred, you know he doesn't like to drive so far from Eastbourne, and you know how upset it makes his sister when he's out late. If Trevor doesn't come quite soon, I think we had better send the car back empty."

"And wait for the ruddy train?" Trevor's father asked wrathfully. "I tell you, Phyllis, if Clapford's not prepared to accept the consequences of running a taxi service, by the Lord Harry, he'd best find himself a new trade."

"Have you ever heard the carolers at St. John's on the first of May?" Mrs. Ashford asked me in a whisper. "They sing from the tower at dawn. It's charming."

It is charming, too. When May came I got up at five o'clock and heard them, though not with Mrs. Ashford. In fact, I never even answered her question. For at that moment, wreathed in smiles, Trevor and Annie appeared below, having finally driven up in the 1938 Morris two-seater which Trevor had managed to borrow for his honeymoon.

"Mum," Annie caroled up, "we're leaving. Come down and see us off."

There was an unseemly scramble down the stairs, led by Annie's mother and Trevor's mother in that order. Aunt Muriel was a strong third. When we reached the sidewalk a kind of orgy of kissing began. Aunt Phyllis, sniffing happily, got so carried away that for a time Mrs. Ashford and I were in danger. At the last minute Annie's father produced an immense sack of confetti from inside his overcoat, and solemnly handed us each a double handful.

"It was a *lovely* party, dears," said Aunt Phyllis, as she kissed Annie.

Then Trevor and Annie were gone in a flurry of colored paper. Within thirty-five seconds Mr. Clapford had his contingent loaded, and shot off toward Eastbourne. Although it's hard to see much through the windows of a moving Humber, especially when there are three women leaning out and waving, I like to think that I got a last glimpse of Aunt Phyllis's husband pulling out his watch to check the time of departure.

When the limousine had got up the street as far as

St. Cat's, I turned around. Mrs. Ashford had vanished. In the gathering darkness Annie's parents and
younger brother stood there in a row on King's Parade looking at me, glum, stoical, expectant. What
they expected I couldn't imagine. Annie's mother
opened her mouth for practically the first time that
day. "Ooo," she said, "wasn't it a good wedding?
My, but we've had a rare spot of fun."

Noah and the scarlet harlot

FOR MANY MONTHS now it has been difficult to walk through a U.S. post office without confronting notices against obscene literature. "Let's stop FILTH through the mails!" one notice urges. "*You* can help fight obscenity," proclaims another, which goes on to explain that the way you can help is by denouncing indecent books to the Government. This one is signed by the Postmaster General himself.

Neither notice gives any very exact definition of what constitutes obscenity. It is not an easy definition to give. Is *Lolita* obscene? I gather that the Postmaster General would say it was. *The Tropic of Capricorn?* Yes, the courts have convicted it. Homer's *Odyssey?* Well, Plato thought so. Just about twenty-three hundred years ago he did a close analysis of the filth in Homer and proceeded to outline a series of revisions that would make the greatest of classical poets fit to read. The Bible? Don't be ridiculous.

Actually, I'm not being ridiculous. I'm simply remembering one of the more colorful passages in the history of American literature. No less an American than Noah Webster regarded the Bible as obscene, a view in which he was warmly seconded by the president and most of the faculty of Yale, who took a resolution to that effect in 1835. The Congregational Church in Connecticut for a time held similar views. If our present Postmaster General reads the Bible, I won't swear that *he* doesn't think it's fairly lascivious.

As for Webster, he not only considered the Bible lascivious—"the utterance of many words and passages of our version is not to be endured," he said flatly in 1833—but he was prepared, in the best Platonic tradition, to undertake its cure. The story of how he played surgeon to the Bible is, I think, one worth telling. It has a certain quaint interest just as a story. Besides that, it has a moral, one which may apply even in our own time, even to current literary healers.

The story begins about the year 1828. Noah Webster was then both an elderly and a very famous man. He had been a judge in Connecticut and one of the founders of a distinguished college in Massachusetts. He was honored throughout the country as the leading American scholar, both for his single-handed revision of American spelling and for his noble array of dictionaries, in recognition of which Yale had recently awarded him an LL.D. He had just that year published in two volumes the first edition of Webster's Unabridged, a work which instantly made Dr. Johnson obsolete and which has been praised for its superb methodology ever since.

The Bible, while it had been and done none of these things, was more elderly and famous still. It had served as the guide of life and the model of literature to several billions of Christians, Webster among them. But it was not, the eminent editor concluded, a suitable book to have around the house. It was "offensive to delicacy and even to decency."

Like those who publish notices *contra obscenitatem* now, he wasn't just thinking of the offense to himself. The Bible as generally printed, Webster said, was not a suitable book to have around *any* nineteenth-century house. It may have been bearable in the remote past, "when men were savage or half-civilized," but for modern men it was just too crude.

Moreover, even as now there were the teen-agers to think of. Many young people of Webster's personal acquaintance—"especially females," he said—were quitting Sunday school because of the Bible. The problem was that their teachers often made them recite from it, and week after week "they are required to read passages which cannot be repeated without a blush."

The solution was obvious and, in fact, Biblical. If thine eye offend thee, pluck it out. If someone else's eye offend thee, pluck that out, too. If it's a book that's causing the offense, censor it. And sometime late in 1828, Webster took yet another horrified look at the Bible and decided that he would. Exactly how he got started is hard to say. But it is reasonable to suppose that he sat down at his desk one winter morning with a copy of the King James Version (*he* called it the Common Version, being a good democrat), with a high-minded attitude, and with a freshly sharpened pencil. The pencil was for making excisions.

The words and passages which Webster found especially unendurable, and which he therefore had in mind to excise, fall into two main classes: New Testament oaths and Old Testament obscenities. In the first class, his chief antagonist was St. Paul. In the second, he had to contend with virtually every prophet the ancient Hebrews produced. It seems fair to assume (or, at least, I choose to) that being a sensible man he took the easier battle first. He opened his New Testament, where he found St. Paul and, just once, St. Luke swearing.

The trouble arose because, like most preachers, St. Paul enjoyed asking rhetorical questions and then answering them himself. "What!" he would ask the Christians of Rome, "shall we sin because we are not under the law but under grace?" And he would answer his own question with Biblical sternness, "God forbid."

With Webster's help, the fierce apostle soon learned to temper his language. "By no means" became his favorite retort to such questions. "Don't do it, fellows," the postal department would probably have him saying now.

Similarly, when Paul found that the Christians at

Corinth were criticizing him and saying he wasn't as
saintly as some of the other saints, he bore down on
them in righteous indignation. "Would to God," he
wrote them, "ye could bear with me a little in *my*
folly [as ye do these other apostles]." "*O that* ye
could bear with me," writes the meek websterized
Paul.

Webster had long ago observed, in his first small
dictionary, that "for men to swear is sinful, dis-
reputable, and odious; but for females or ladies to
swear appears more abominable and scandalous."
For saints to swear must have been beyond even the
Websterian capacity to censure. It is fortunate that
they can be broken of the habit.

Prophets are another matter altogether. Though
relatively indifferent to oaths, they seem to have a
universal addiction to earthy language. The result is
that when Webster laid aside the New Testament
and opened the Old, he was committing himself to
a struggle of epic proportions. Wherever he turned
he found indecency rampant. The ancient prophets
ran to extremes in every direction. They seemed to
know only two classes of women: virgins and whores.
They could hardly speak of either without making
some gratuitous reference to virgin breasts or whorish
wombs. If they turned their attention to men, they
always found some excuse to mention buttocks and
privy members. Babies in the Old Testament seemed
to do nothing but suckle, once they had come out of
the belly. The very fish in Old Testament rivers
couldn't die without some prophet's waxing lyrical
over the smell.

With a pure heart and a large stock of euphemisms, Webster plunged into this mess. And at first the cleansing seemed to go easily. As he looked through the opening book, Genesis, he found the Lord Jehovah opening and closing an occasional womb, and he found one Jacob accusing his sons Simeon and Levi of making him "stink" among the Canaanites. He also found Onan practicing onanism by spilling his seed on the ground, and Onan's sister-in-law playing the harlot (with Onan's father) and being with child by whoredom.

It was absurdly easy to correct all this. A junior postal clerk could have done it. In Genesis websterized, the Lord Jehovah makes women *fruitful* or *barren* rather than opening or closing their wombs. Jacob accuses his sons Simeon and Levi of having made him *odious* among the Canaanites. Onan no longer spills seed; he *frustrates purposes*. And Tamar, while she still plays the harlot, now is with child by *lewdness*, rather than by Onan's father.

The second book, Exodus, went just as swimmingly. Here Webster found additional stinking, to be sure. For example, when the Lord promised Moses to strike at the Egyptians through their national water supply, He did it in these words: "And the fish that is in the river shall die, and the river shall stink; and the Egyptians shall lothe to drink of the water of the river." A few chapters further on, the Israelites, now safely out of Egypt and feeding on manna, complained that they lothed to eat the stuff if it had been kept overnight, because "it bred worms and stank."

It took only moderate ingenuity to make the Lord

tell Moses that the river would become "offensive in smell," and to make the children of Israel discover that overripe manna merely "putrefied."

The only other problem in all Exodus is the wording of a command the Lord gives Moses to keep the Israelites away from strange gods. Using what was apparently one of His favorite verbs (or a favorite, at any rate, with the fifty-four scholars who produced the King James Version), the Lord tells Moses to keep a sharp eye on the local Amorites and Canaanites. If left unmolested, He warns, they are sure "to go a whoring" after their tribal deities.

Worse yet, the Lord continues, you Israelites will very likely "take of their daughters unto thy sons, and their daughters [will] go a whoring after their gods, and make thy sons go a whoring after their gods." Under Webster's reproving eye, the Lord moderates His language. Be careful, He contents Himself with saying, lest thy sons and daughters-in-law "go astray."

But the further Webster ventured into the Old Testament, the harder his task became. He continued, certainly, to cope with minor problems. When the Lord issued a command to the priests of Israel not to "take a wife that is a whore or profane" ("a harlot or vile prostitute," says the Douai Version, the leading Catholic Bible in English), Webster deftly substituted "lewd woman." When Ezekiel thundered against the two symbolic sisters of Judea that "they committed whoredoms in Egypt; they committed whoredoms in their youth . . . and there they bruised the teats of their virginity," Webster toned him down to saying that they committed "lewd deeds" in Egypt and in their youth, and there were they "first corrupted." By contrast, the most distinguished of recent Protestant Bibles, the Revised Standard Version of 1952, says forthrightly that there were their "virgin bosoms handled."

With equal diligence, Webster reduced the woman Hannah in the Book of Samuel from giving her son suck to the more refined act of nursing him. He changed the lewd "buttocks" of the Egyptians into their decorous "hind-parts." He demoted to a mere maid servant the lively "wench" who brought the news from Jonathan to King David. And to the hungry Israelites who once were permitted by Moses to lust after meat, he gave the right merely to "desire" it.

But the prophets were irrepressible. Trying to cleanse them by blue-penciling was like trying to put out a forest fire by stamping on it barefoot. Before Noah reached much over halfway through the Old Testament, he virtually gave up. "It was my wish to make some further alterations," he wrote sadly at the end of his preface, "but difficulties occurred which I could not well remove."

That was putting the case mildly. Some of the "difficulties" were several chapters long, and as for the Song of Solomon, the whole book constitutes one. In fact, here Webster abandoned his reform completely. King Solomon's torrential passages of love, with whatever inward wincings, he reprinted verbatim, merely correcting the syntax. In the second chapter he even managed to make things worse.

"Stay me with flagons, comfort me with apples, for I am sick of love," wrote Solomon. The verse seems to suggest that those who commit lewd acts wind up in a state of acute boredom, their only remaining desire a craving for fresh fruit. Webster dispelled that illusion at once. "You are sick *with* love," he firmly corrected King Solomon, thus making it clear that the great monarch's distress arose from a lack of lewdness rather than from too much of it.

Once past the majestic indecency of Solomon, Webster did revive slightly, it's true. He canceled several wombs in Jeremiah. He abated a stink (caused by the heathen) in Joel to an *odious scent* and another in Amos to an *ill savor*. He changed the scarlet whore of Babylon to a scarlet harlot—Webster's harlot scarlet, possibly, because like the Sunday school children she was blushing at her own behavior. But it was obvious that the heart had gone out of his reforms. As a true obscenity fighter he failed miserably, and he knew it. The Bible was a book to shock postmasters before he made his corrections, and it remained a book to shock postmasters afterwards.

Unkindest cut of all, "The Holy Bible in the Common Version, With Amendments of the Language by Noah Webster, LL.D." didn't even sell well—at least not compared, say, to the King James Version, which has been through several thousand editions, or the Douai Version, of which a hundred million or so copies exist. Durrie & Peck of New Haven, Connecticut, published Webster's Bible in 1833. They ran off their third and last edition in 1841, two years before the author died. No one has reprinted it since.

The Congregational Church of Connecticut, which had semi-officially adopted the book in the mid-thirties, dropped it again. Yale quietly forgot about its endorsement. Today the King James, which minces so few words, and the Douai and Revised Standard Versions, which mince none, rule supreme, even in Connecticut. Copies of all three pass through U.S. post offices continually, often en route to clergymen of the highest probity.

Today in the best pulpits Job still hurls out from his misery the great, defiant questions, "Why died I not from the womb? why did I not give up the ghost when I came out of the belly? Why did the knees prevent me? or why the breasts that I should give suck?" instead of asking more modestly, as Webster had taught him, "Why did I not expire at the time of my birth?"

Today the Psalmist still heaps imprecations on Israel for "thy whoredoms with thy lovers," instead of reproaching in a more civilized, Websterian way her "carnal connections" with these lovers. And to this day the scarlet whore (or harlot) of New Testament Revelations remains "drunk with the wine of her fornication," and not simply intoxicated with "lewdness." In short, despite the best efforts of the most distinguished bowdlerizer America has yet produced, the Bible retains its earthy flavor and its vaulting poetry. It may even be, though I hardly like to suggest it, that the two are not entirely separable. At any rate, it is clear that Webster could not and the American public would not separate them. Not even with the support of Yale. Probably not even if the then Postmaster General had pitched in.

"Wherefore," as the prophet Isaiah somewhat indelicately put it, and as I grossly echo him, "my bowels shall sound like an harp for Moab, and mine inward parts for Kir-haresh."

The pigeon-kickers
of Morningside Heights

KICKING PIGEONS is considerably harder than most people suppose. It is also more commendable, at least in cities.

As a native of New York, a city yet richer in pigeons than London, I sensed even as a child the general desirability of taking action against these too-friendly birds. The front of the tall brownstone house in which we lived was streaked with perpetual festoons of dirty white, each marking a pigeon's favored roost, and it was a rash child who went bareheaded on our sidewalk, especially at sunset.

Our family maid, a colored girl who had come to New York from the South, never really learned to look before she sat, and her expressions of annoyance on discovering that she had been preceded on some park bench by a pigeon grew, if anything, stronger with the years. Doubtless my own attitude was influenced by her passionate Virginia outcries.

But in those days the possibility of counter-pigeon work seemed remote. The pigeons were many, and they had powerful allies in the people who stood in Father Duffy Square feeding them bread crumbs out of brown paper bags. My father once spoke of smuggling down a dozen peregrine falcons from Canada, but this was mere passing irritation, caused by an unfortunate accident to a new suit and forgotten after my mother hustled it off to the cleaners. A good thing, too. A few years later, when a pigeonthrope on Twelfth Street began putting out poisoned grain, there was a commotion in the papers hardly equaled since the assassination of President McKinley. The man was eventually caught and, I believe, given a savage sentence to jail.

It was not until I was nearly grown and my nurse had long since married and returned to Virginia (where the dominant birds are turkey buzzards: solemn, anxious creatures who keep to themselves, and wouldn't know a park bench if they saw one) that an avenue of anti-pigeon work opened up for me. I met at a party the Senior Boot of the Columbia University Pigeon-Kickers Club. We discovered almost at once our common distaste, and I received that same evening an invitation to become a guest member of the club.

The C.U. Pigeon-Kickers, whose name appears in no official University record, then consisted of some thirty undergraduates and of half a dozen outsiders like myself. The founders, it was said, were a group of young sculptors and architectural students at Columbia almost forty years ago, men moved to action by the gradual disappearance of New York's statuary under a coating of pigeon-droppings. Some of the members I knew twenty-five years later were still moved by a protective feeling toward statues and Doric columns. Others were motivated more personally, for Morningside Heights, upon which Columbia stands, is a major pigeon stronghold, and he who lives there is likely to become encrusted. A handful of the members may simply have enjoyed kicking pigeons.

The club met once a month to discuss strategy, which ran as far afield as the recurrent plan of one of our sculptors to flood the city with mechanical pigeons, complete with metal feathers and a recorded coo. Each would be designed to peck up bread crumbs in a realistic manner, up to some very large number, and then to fly straight to a special Department of Sanitation depot. There the crumbs would be removed and the empty pigeons turned back into the city. One would thus, the sculptor insisted, satisfy the benevolence of the people with the brown paper bags while sparing the fine St. Gaudens statue of Admiral Farragut, not to mention Charles Keck's more modest image of Father Duffy, right there in Duffy Square. One would even, he was convinced, be taking a first step toward making outdoor cafés practicable. But all this was just theory. The actual work of the club consisted, of course, of kicking, and that we did not in conclave but alone. It was, in fact, an absolute requirement of the club that the first pigeon of a new member be taken unaccompanied, and it was a measure of our honesty that the candidate's account of this solitary ordeal was always accepted without question.

My own first pigeon was perhaps typical. I got him in the middle of a spring afternoon in 1947, while I was home on vacation from the New England college I then attended. I'd already made a number of furtive attempts, but pigeons are not easy to kick. Like most birds, they seem to possess a kind of internal radar or Distant Early Warning System; and even when they are facing away from you and obviously much occupied with their own affairs, they can feel your foot coming and scoot out of the way. Yes, and an even greater barrier than the animal cunning of the birds themselves is the instant hostility raised in most people by the sight of a pigeon-kicker at work. It is this hostility which makes the club's work so risky, which requires that we do it in seclusion, and which gives us our panache.

On the afternoon mentioned, I was walking across East Fortieth Street on my way home from a wedding reception. Between First and Second Avenues I came on a patch of very messy sidewalk and a small flock of pigeons milling around on it. One, a large male, had his ruff extended and his two lecherous eyes fixed on separate willing females. He was engaged in making that revolting noise which to a pigeon means come-hither. Clearly he had no thought for me. I glanced swiftly about; the street for once was deserted. I drew back my foot and aimed a magnificent kick.

Even during the very height and madness of courtship the male pigeon had kept his radar running, however, and just before my foot made contact he sensed its arrival and began a rapid dash forward, squawking loudly. This of course mitigated the force of my blow, and the net effect was to provide him with an assisted take-off of an undignified but painless nature. Still, you could see that he didn't like it. The experience would, I felt, give him a reason for considering a change of residence. To induce the city's pigeons to move to Philadelphia or at least out as far as Scarsdale was our avowed purpose in the Pigeon-Kickers.

I was contemplating his indignant retreating form with some satisfaction when it happened. A truck driver emerged from the doorway in which he had been lighting his cigar and addressed me.

"Did I see you kick dat little bird?" he demanded in a terrible voice.

"If you mean that pigeon, I was feeding it," I said hastily. In moments of panic I tend not only to lie but to lie very unconvincingly.

"I seen you kick dat little bird," the truck driver repeated, pounding a massive fist against the great palm of his other hand for emphasis.

The remark did not seem to invite an answer. In any event, it was obvious that both logic and casuistry would fail with the fellow. I started running. The truck driver gave chase. In fact he thundered after me all the way to Fifth Avenue—or at least I didn't see fit to stop running until I had reached its familiar purlieus and stood panting in front of the Public Library. A small pigeon who was quietly molting on the back of one of the superb stone lions that guard the Library steps eyed me curiously. I smiled at him with false benevolence and slipped off in the direction of the Frick Collection.

During my formal initiation, which took place that June, the lecherous male was entered in the club books as the 2,487th of his breed to receive a monitory toe. Before I grew too old for the work—twenty-two is the normal age limit—I added three others to the total. To the best of my belief, a dedicated band of younger men carry on the labor to this very day.

But against the city's formidable array of pigeons and pigeon-feeders the club has thus far won no real victory. It rains and still the sea is salt. It rains, and even on Morningside Heights itself still the statuary is blotched, the parked automobile spotted, the careless pedestrian in danger. The time has come for a larger anti-pigeon campaign, one that will encompass not only all of New York, but London and Venice as well.

Often one hears it said that there is an absence of adventure in cities, that the young in particular can find no worth-while risks to run, no strenuous way to work for the public good. That's nonsense, a claim as stale as the crusts of bread the old are forever pulling out of those brown paper bags. Let them kick pigeons.

The winning of Susan Appleby

OFF AND ON for a year, ever since I first saw it,
I've been worrying about an advertisement put out
by one of the women's magazines. It was a huge cartoon, really, and what it showed was a good-looking
young man seated on a motorcycle. He is pulled up
in front of a suburban house, one of those substantial
houses with plenty of lawn that you can see at a
glance belongs to an upper-middle-class family.
About six feet away from him is standing a pretty girl
who has obviously just come out to meet him. I think
they must have a date to go to a Junior League dance,
because along with his crash helmet and motorcycle
gloves the young man is wearing a tuxedo, while the
girl has on a low-cut black dress and a sort of man-

tilla. She is staring in wild disbelief at the motorcycle, as if she hadn't previously known such things existed. One dainty hand is raised in consternation to her mouth. Obviously she is about to invent a headache and rush back inside. Tomorrow she will demand a formal apology.

Underneath this cartoon was a piece of text. "Where women are concerned," it said, "the 'vehicle' you choose to carry your message makes all the difference in the world. Would you woo a lady on a motorcycle?" The implication seems to be, try it and you'll die a bachelor.

The more I study that ad, the more I keep thinking of my cousin Susan Appleby, who as it happens *was* wooed on a motorcycle. She also chances to be a lady. In fact, hers is a story remarkably similar to the one suggested by the cartoon, all except for the way it ends.

Susan, who was brought up in an atmosphere of Chryslers and Lincolns—her father is a doctor—was famous from infancy for her ladylike ways. At three she could drop a curtsy. At eight she designed an evening dress for one of her dolls. At eleven she owned her first mantilla. The Christmas she was sixteen I happened to tell her an amusing story that had been going the rounds at college, where I was then a sophomore. So far from being grateful, she gave me a reproachful look. "Why, Cousin Noel!" she exclaimed, blushing delicately. "That borders on the lewd."

Two years later Susan herself went off to college, to Radcliffe; and though not herself a New Englander or even from the East, she soon began cutting a swath through the better circles at Harvard. At least once, her mother has told my Aunt Phoebe, she was wooed, and quite persistently, too, on the front seat of a Jaguar owned by the richest undergraduate in Massachusetts. (Naturally she was too much of a lady to succumb.) Her senior year, however, Susan met a graduate student at Tufts named Stanley Bates, Jr., who owned a Harley-Davidson motorcycle. The attraction was mutual and instantaneous.

Lady that she was, Susan at first refused to go within fifty feet of Stanley's motorcycle, much less be wooed on it. "Nasty, dirty thing," she is supposed to have said. "No self-respecting girl would be seen on one." She hinted that he ought to sell it. When Stanley refused, they had a terrible fight which ended only when he agreed to park two blocks away from her dormitory whenever he came to get her, and to walk up to the dorm swinging a set of car keys in his hand. They would then sneak down to the corner and take a taxi.

The climax of this unnatural courtship came early in the third month after they met. At the time their future looked dark. Stanley was depressed because Susan refused to be wooed in the backs of taxis, either. ("Stanley! He can see us in the mirror," she would say, pulling her hands free.) Susan, on the other hand, was alarmed to find herself falling in love with a man who not only rode motorcycles but whose parents might operate a roller-skating rink, for all she knew. All Stanley had ever said was that they lived in Worcester.

One night as they were starting in to the theater in Boston by cab, she asked Stanley point-blank why he had never invited her home to meet them. Stanley gave her a dark look. "You won't ride on the machine, babe," he said, "and these damn taxis run into money."

"Silly," said Susan, "we can take the *train*. Maybe we could even persuade your mother to meet us at the station."

Stanley agreed that this was possible, and a date was set for the trip. Naturally Susan had many questions to ask about how to behave and what to wear, but Stanley would answer practically none of them. Even when they were on the train, Susan in a quiet black dress, small hat, and doeskin gloves, he kept up his maddening silence. "I want it to be a surprise for you," he said.

It was. Mrs. Bates was duly waiting at the station, and when Susan saw in what, only her innate good breeding kept her from hurling herself back on the train and proceeding to Albany. Ladies endure what they must, though, and instead she stepped gallantly into the sidecar. She even managed to smile at Mrs. Bates. Stanley hopped in next to her. His mother gunned the huge motorcycle, and they tore off down the station plaza. Susan was terrified. She clearly wasn't going to hold on to Stanley, and so, clean gloves or no, she was forced to clutch the grimy seat with both hands for the entire trip. Conversation was out of the question. Only when Mrs. Bates zipped to a halt in front of a big eighteenth-century house and turned off the engine was she able to let go. Then, furiously ignoring Stanley's arm, she clambered out by herself and marched up to the front door. She wouldn't even let Stanley hold it open for her. "Beast," she hissed. "You planned this."

Stanley took her coat.

Mrs. Bates joined them in the living room. "I'm delighted you could come, Susan," she said, unsnapping her helmet. "Usually I meet Stanley's friends in the car, but when he wrote us that you were Girls' Racing Champion of Wisconsin and the daughter of a former International, I knew I'd better bring the machine. We're an old motorcycling family ourselves."

"How nice for you," said Susan, giving Stanley a look that would have wilted a stack of women's magazines five feet high. "And does Mr. Bates ride professionally?"

"Why, no, he's with an engineering firm," his wife said apologetically. "Bates and Rydzewski, here in Worcester. They design factories."

"Small factories," said Stanley.

"But he hasn't always been so stuffy," Mrs. Bates continued. "When I first met him, he had a motorcycle act with Ringling Brothers. You know, the old stunt where you ride perpendicularly around the inside of a circular ring."

"I'm afraid I don't know," said Susan, her voice like winter on the Great Lakes.

But Mrs. Bates didn't hear. She was smiling reminiscently. "The times we had with that motorcycle," she said. "We were with the circus three years, and my husband changed the act five times. I guess that summer with the tiger was the worst."

"Tiger?" asked Susan. "I thought Mr. Bates was riding a motorcycle around a ring."

"He was. But the year after we were married he took it into his head to buy this old tiger named Freddie and train it to ride in a child's wagon hitched on behind. I must say, the crowds went wild."

"So did Mother," said Stanley. "Freddie was a traumatic experience for her."

"Well, that tiger was such a big baby," Mrs. Bates explained. "He was always coddling himself. I remember the day of our first wedding anniversary, he caught a little cold—just a sniffle—but would he go on? Certainly not. He spent the evening comfortably asleep in his cage, and I celebrated my wedding anniversary by being sewed in a tiger skin and hauled around in that wagon. I didn't speak to my husband for three days."

It was at this point, Susan has told me, that she decided to quit going out with men altogether and to spend her life at home in Wisconsin taking care of her parents. If it hadn't been for the happy accident, she might well have done it, instead of marrying Stanley and spending her honeymoon in Mexico learning to drive scooters. I won't get into the details of how she drank too much champagne with dinner in an effort to forget that tiger skin, and how she and Stanley missed the last train, and how he tricked her onto his father's old circus machine.

It is enough to say that when from her position on the pillion and in her drunken state, she instinctively wrapped both arms around Stanley to keep from falling off, a feeling of pure femaleness coursed through her that ladies aren't supposed to know about. She should have let go the moment she felt it, I grant you. But if a lady lets go on a moving motorcycle, she winds up in the ditch. Susan wound up holding on tighter—and about three months later marrying Stanley. The last time I saw her she was wearing a Mexican leather jacket and tailored jodhpurs, and stunning she looked, too.

Would you woo a lady (char, sales, bearded, or actual) on a motorcycle? I'll say only this: It's a poor idea unless you're prepared to win her. Ladies that you're just dallying with you'd better take for a ride in a Cadillac or buy a copy of some nice women's magazine for.

The title game

A COLLEGE FRIEND of mine has lately become, at thirty-four, one of the vice-presidents of a large corporation. "Vice-president" is defined in the dictionary that goes with his office as the man "next in rank below a president, acting as president in case of that officer's absence or disability." Nevertheless, sharing his post with him, he has calculated, are two senior vice-presidents, fourteen other ordinary vice-presidents, and eleven assistant vice-presidents. His tabulation does not include the twenty-seven vice-presidents of subsidiary companies who happen not to be also vice-presidents of the parent corporation.

"This damn outfit is getting to be like an Irish monastery," complains Fred, who majored in medieval history. He's referring to the fact that in the early Middle Ages the ecclesiastical hierarchy of Ireland was notably top-heavy. When St. Mochta was abbot of Louth, for example, along in the sixth century, he used to sit down to dinner with a hundred bishops, who were his executive assistants and subordinates— his vice-abbots, you might say—in running the place. Abbots of other, smaller monasteries, like Moville and Clonmacnoise, had squads of twenty or thirty bishops on hand, each with his private cell, miter, tunicle, and right to be called *Beatissimus*. About all they lacked were dioceses.

There's a certain aptness to Fred's comparison— which, incidentally, he has repeated all around the company, thus gaining himself a useful reputation as a man of culture. All the same, I think that with the usual arrogance of the businessman he is trying to claim for his own kind a practice which is in fact common to the entire United States. We're *all* lavish with titles. One of the stirring sights of our time is to watch the undertakers soaring into morticians and respectable handymen blossoming out as mainte- nance engineers. My kind, who are college teachers, have managed matters better still.

Starting with the original title of "professor," which used to belong to a handful of distinguished old men, we have extended its glories to include nearly all of us, by the simple invention of the title "associate pro- fessor" for those who aren't really professors, and "as- sistant professor" for those who aren't even associates. All are impartially addressed as "Professor." Our stu- dents generously carry the process one step further.

Down below the assistants are the instructors, including me, a group who in a monastery would rank about equal to lay brothers. Three-quarters of our students, when passing us on campus, greet us with a cheery "Hi, Professor." The remaining quarter, more formal-minded, simper, "Good morning, Doctor." Most of us have no Ph.D.

Find me the corporation executive who fares as well as that. Furthermore, I think I know a better analogy than Fred's. It's not sixth-century Ireland that America is getting to be like, but twentieth-century Portugal. Portugal, so conservative in other ways, is very forward-looking in the matter of titles and modes of address, and I think its example is the one democratic men will choose to follow. The Portuguese grasped some time ago the principle that it is no good simply having lots of bishops or gradually extending professorships down to the women who run play schools. What's needed is a system of honorifics that will take in all living people. Theirs does. Equally important, it should work as well in common speech as it does on office doors. After all, Fred isn't yet *called* "Mr. Vice-President," much less *Beatissimus*. He's called Fred. He would not be in Portugal. Finally, the perfectly inflated system, while honoring all, should still leave some room for subtle variation, so that if you know your way around you can distinguish a senior vice-president from an office boy merely by how he is addressed. The Portuguese system has more subtle variations than there are gambits in chess.

Take, just as a starter, the form you use for servants

in Portugal, which is Your Grace, or *Vossa Mercê*. No one can say this isn't polite. "Will Your Grace pass the peas?" as a command from mistress to maid seems unexceptionable. Moreover, it has five distinct variations, all meaningful. The full *Vossa Mercê* would perhaps only be used in speaking to a butler at a formal dinner party (or by a senior vice-president to an office boy, and in Tiffany's, since it is also correct for subordinates in office and the better class of tradespeople). For lesser servants one would shorten it either to *Vossemecê* or the curt *Vocemecê*. Both still mean "Your Grace," they're just less honorific. *Vocemecê* even has its own separate abbreviation for use in writing, so that if you were leaving notes in the house for both the butler and the parlormaid, you'd begin the butler's *V.M.ê* and the parlormaid's *Vm.ê*

"Your Grace" can be shortened still further, to either *Vòmecê* or *Você* (*V.ê*), but as Professor Joseph Dunn says in that superb Portuguese grammar which I am using as a final authority, these two forms "are still more familiar, and are used only in addressing workmen and among men who are intimate friends." A Tiffany clerk addressed as *Você* would probably refuse to serve you. At the very least, he might neglect to call you the *Vossa Excelência* form of Your Excellency, which is the usual well-bred way of speaking to strangers in Portugal. He might use the casual *Vossência* form, or he might even be impudent and just call you "the gentleman." The one thing you can be sure of is that he wouldn't call you "you," since the Portuguese normally reserve *that* for animals and inanimate objects.

It would be a mistake to assume that servants and strangers get some kind of exceptional treatment in Portugal—that I am picking extreme cases. All Portuguese fare well. If you were sending a note to a mail-order clerk at the Lisbon equivalent of Gimbels, you would begin it *Vossa Senhoria,* which translates "Your Lordship." If you were the twenty-eighth vice-president of a Portuguese bank, and you were playing bridge with a few other corporate officers and their wives, and you wanted to ask one of the wives if she had seen *The Music Man,* you would say, "*Vossa Excelência viu o espectáculo, minha senhora?*" This comes out, "Your Excellency, has she seen the play, my lady?" Or if you were this same vice-president, and on very good terms with your secretary, you might ask her, "*a senhora Dona Luísa tem um lápis?*" which would correctly be translated, "Louise, have you got a pencil?" Word-for-word, of course, it's "Has Madam the Lady Louise a pencil?" And so throughout the country.

Some system like this, as I say, is what I think we're slowly working toward in the United States. We've a long way to go, of course. Here an industrial protection consultant (ex-plant guard), there two police officers (there *are* no non-officers on American police forces), yonder a herd of professors—we make our progress piecemeal. Still, it's possible to take a peek at our eventual goal. It's not only possible, it's irresistible, and I have done so. The time is a good many years hence. Fred, now the senior vice-president of his company, is driving a rented car from the airport near Davenport, Iowa, down to the company's new plant in Wapello. Just outside Davenport he stops to pick up a man whose car has broken down.

FRED: Hop in, Your Excellency. I'm going as far as Wapello.

MAN: Gee, that's swell. Your Excellency could let me out in Muscatine.

FRED: What kind of work does Your Excellency do?

MAN: I'm Fifth Assistant Contractor on a house-building operation. In the old days we used to call it being a carpenter.

FRED: Times have sure changed, haven't they? I can remember when I was a boy, Senior Executive Food Handlers, Type Two, were called butchers.

MAN: Excellency! That word! There's such a thing as being *too* frank.

FRED: Sorry, Your Grace. Sometimes I get carried away. We corporation vice-presidents do.

MAN: Superexcellency! I didn't know. Forgive me, Your Management.

At this point a siren is heard. Fred pulls over on the shoulder.

COP: Let me see Your Excellency's license and registration. Does the gentleman realize he was going eighty miles an hour?

FRED: Officer, Your Patrolship is much mistaken if he thinks I was doing eighty. Perhaps his radar set needs adjusting.

COP: Tell it to the judge, Excellency.

MAN: Excuse me, Your Management. I'll get out here.

The cop escorts Fred to the office of the local J.P.,

*who examines first Fred's license and, very carefully,
all his credit cards.*

J.P.:   Hmm, thirty miles over the limit . . . reckless driving . . . unauthorized passenger . . . could
be a pretty serious charge.

FRED: How serious?

J.P.:   Revoked license, Your Management, and
probably at least a two hundred dollar fine.

FRED: My Lord Chief Justice of the Peace, this is
absurd. Can't we work out some kind of good old
American compromise?

J.P.:   I won't say no. Tell Your Management what.
I see his company has a grooming-products division
in Des Moines.

FRED (*hastily*):   That has nothing to do with me.

J.P. (*persisting*):   My daughter Emmy's a graduate beautician—got her B.A. in coiffeurage, her M.A.
in fingernails, and everything. What about some con-
sulting work for the kid? Know what I mean, give her
a nice little monthly check?

FRED: Your Honor overestimates my influence in
the company. Her Beautyhood his daughter would
have to see the Right Prosperous the Chairman of
the Board.

J.P.:   Aah, forget it. Maybe Your Sub-Manage-
ment has a better idea.

FRED: Well, as a matter of fact, I was just about
to say that we senior executives have a Corporate
Donation Fund. I'd be glad to see that fifty dollars
went to Your Honor's favorite charity. And, of course,
twenty-five to His Patrolship's.

J.P.: Let's say a hundred for me and fifty for His Patrolship.

FRED: What about sixty and thirty, and two honorary memberships in our new V-P Club of Wapello? Title goes with the office.

J.P.: What title?

FRED: Why, Vice-President, Division of External Relations; Member, Management Advisory Committee; Teammate, Iowa Executive Team. Forget the sixty and thirty, and I might even be able to pick up a couple of honorary Bus.D.'s from our corporate university.

J.P.: Your Top Management is a real square shooter. I accept.

COP: So do I. Permit me to give Your Munificence a police escort to Wapello.

Nuclear disobedience

THIS ESSAY is going to be a little bit embarrassing in its present company, like a Jehovah's Witness who has strayed into an Episcopal picnic. He *will* preach. The Episcopalians may like what the fellow says, but he's too earnest for them: he keeps waving his arms and making the same point over and over, long after the entire audience has grasped it, committed it to memory, and possibly tried repeating it backwards in rhymed couplets. If only he'd sit down and eat a deviled egg, and stop all that shouting, they could get on with the day's activities.

As it happens, I am an Episcopalian myself, and very fond of picnics. Normally I would sympathize with the other essays and be on their side against this one. Even as it is, I won't blame them much if they crowd back along the page and glower. But for once I am constrained to play the sweating Witness.

What I have to witness is the familiar fact that the United States possesses weapons which are too powerful for it to control, and which may at any time destroy us and the world, without anyone's ever quite having meant to. We all know about our danger, and just as soon as our government and the Russian government (and, of course, the Chinese, French, and British governments) reach an agreement to disarm, we will all breathe a huge sigh of relief, and maybe give up smoking. So we weren't to be extinguished after all.

Meanwhile, progress toward such an agreement is imperceptible, and the danger increases. What does any man do to avert it? Well, some write letters to newspapers, and some distribute leaflets. Some go to see their Congressman, and urge that the United States should renounce its nuclear bombs now, or at least stop testing, whether Russia does or not. (The Congressman, if he is typical, explains that this would be bad politics.) A few daring ones sail their boats into the test areas or picket missile bases, and they are ignored or quietly put in jail. Most of us wait with a mixture of hope and resignation for our government to do something, and pray that extinction doesn't come first. And while we wait, we help to increase the danger. As Air Force officers, we fly live bombs over the Arctic, and sometimes over the towns where our children lie sleeping. As physicists we design new and worse weapons. As technicians we build them. As administrators we plan them. As taxpayers we pay for them. And we don't know what else we can do. For surely if there were anything, our government would tell us, or the people would rise with a thunderous voice and tell the government.

The worst of it is that those of us who write the letters and plead with the Congressmen actually have a feeling of virtue. We tell ourselves that we are doing all a single man can do, and if we die in a nuclear blast it won't be our fault. Some of us think in our heart of hearts that whatever happens to the others, we won't die in one—it would be too unfair. At the last minute, we secretly feel, some god will step out of the machine and rescue those of us who protested. Or at least one ought to.

Henry Thoreau, from whose essay "Civil Disobedience" I take my text, has something to say about this feeling. He was talking, a hundred and twelve years ago, about those Americans who knew in their souls that slavery was wrong and who wished to see it ended. "They hesitate and they regret," says Thoreau, "and sometimes they petition; but they do nothing in earnest and with effect. They will wait, well disposed, for others to remedy the evil, that they may no longer have it to regret. At most, they give only a cheap vote, and a feeble countenance and God-speed, to the right, as it goes by them." Such as these, says Thoreau, "command no more respect than men of straw or a lump of dirt." So much for our sense of virtue in that we wrote a letter or signed a petition. Men of flesh have to take stronger action than that.

There's another problem, of course, and Thoreau

deals with that, too. It is hard for a single person *to* take much action, in a country like the United States. Solitary action seems undemocratic. As Thoreau puts it, "Men generally, under such a government as this, think that they ought to wait until they have persuaded the majority. . . ." If a minority of us know that we must renounce nuclear weapons here and now, while we still can, and the majority hasn't yet realized it, then our job is to educate and persuade the majority. And how are we to do it, except with letters and petitions and television shows, and other harmless expressions of opinion?

On all expedient matters, Thoreau would agree with this view, and so must any good citizen. On matters of total conscience, such as slavery and the use of radiation, another and a harder rule applies. In matters of total conscience, men sometimes have to disobey the government and the half-felt will of the majority. Indeed, the disobedience of conscientious men may provide the only means through which the majority can find its true will. The thunderous voice of the people has its first origin in the stubborn throats of just such men. Silence them, and there is no check left on government but the opinion poll, which is no check at all. Thoreau puts the case more succinctly. In matters of total conscience, he says, "any man more right than his neighbors constitutes a majority of one already." As this special kind of majority, it is his plain duty to act.

What this means in the United States now, it seems to me, is that those who care whether humanity survives must begin to risk something more than their

signatures on a petition. Those of us who fly live
bombs could always try refusing. Those of us who
build them could look for other work. Those of us
who are reservists in the armed forces—and I am
one myself—could serve notice that we will not fight
in a nuclear war. (That very few of us would have a
chance to fight, our chief role, like that of other people, being to perish, is for the moment beside the
point. So is the fact that we seem just as likely to
end our species in a peaceful accident as in war.)
Those of us who finance this petard with which we
are to hoist ourselves could even try not paying our
taxes. It would be interesting to see what happened
if two or three hundred thousand of us did refuse to
pay next year.

There would be a special rightness in Americans
doing these things. As much as anyone, we are responsible for letting the weapon out of control in the
first place. Our technology and our genius built it,
our money paid for it. We were the ones who took an
atomic bomb which, in order to serve warning on
Japan, we could perhaps have dropped in the open
sea off Yokohama or into one of the great inland
forests, and released its radiation onto a city full of
human beings. Three days later, while the Japanese
were deciding whether or not to surrender, we repeated the act on another city. In 1961 Japanese are
still dying of leukemia as a result. There is a chance
that for the rest of history some Japanese babies will
be monstrously mutated as a result. We did that.

That the Japanese would almost certainly have
loosed radiation on our cities in 1945, if they had had

the bombs, is no counterargument. We are the ones who did do it, and in consequence we have a little more atomic responsibility than anyone else. Decent Germans must feel a special concern for Israel, because of the Jews Germany slaughtered, and decent Israelis must be concerned for Palestine Arabs, because of the land Israel has taken. Decent Americans must feel that concern for the entire human race, insofar as we have threatened its health and its survival with our free use of radiation. Possibly we had to do what we did in 1945. Possibly we have to be the ones to stop now. Even self-interest suggests that. After all, anyone who believes that the Japanese would have used nuclear weapons on us in 1945, supposing they'd had them, must believe that some day the English, the French, the Russians, the Cubans, our surviving Indians *will* use them on us. Anyone who believes that and who does not push in earnest and with effect toward disarmament is a fool.

One more point needs to be brought up, and I want to beat the reader to it. The point is simply whether all this talk about extinction unless the world gives up nuclear weapons isn't rather alarmist. After all, we Episcopalians have been going on our picnics for years, and we haven't been washed out yet. People have always been claiming that the world was about to come to an end, unless this or that was done, and they have been wrong every single time. Our government assures us they are wrong this time—and would probably add that those who refuse to fly live bombs or pay their taxes will most assuredly go to jail.

I like to imagine a council of Blackfoot Indians

about the year 1800. They are discussing a rumor that white men are slowly moving west, and that they have with them a terrible new weapon that shoots fire. Certain alarmists on the council predict disaster.

"Pooh," answer the rest. "People said that when the bow-and-arrow was invented. Remember when those other white men came up from Mexico on horses? We had never seen horses, and you hysterical types were running around moaning that all was lost. Remember, we told you we'd get our own horses and restore the balance of power? Well, didn't we? Don't be so excitable. You'll be predicting the end of buffalo next."

Ask the surviving Blackfoot Indians whether or not their world came to an end.

I also like to imagine an informal conclave of Neanderthal hunters about the year 74,000 B.C. They are discussing a new kind of flint spear used by the Cro-Magnons in the most recent fight. Certain alarmists among the hunters predict disaster.

"Pooh," answer the rest. "People said that when the throwing stick was invented. We'll get our own flint spears and restore the balance of power. Too dangerous? You'd rather make a treaty? Listen, we'd rather run a little risk than make a treaty with those damn Cro-Magnons. What do you want to do, compromise the Neanderthal way of life? You'll be predicting the end of mammoths next."

As the Neanderthals were entirely wiped out ("Evidence from Krapina in Croatia," wrote Professor Hooton of Harvard, "indicates in no uncertain terms that the Neanderthaloids in this region were eaten

by their more highly evolved successors."); since
Neanderthals are extinct, it is difficult to question
them. But ask their ghosts whether or not their world
came to an end.

The only difference now is that with radiation we
can all die together, instead of some doing the wiping
out and some the surviving. Or even if there should
be survivors of the nuclear war or the nuclear mistake, what guarantee has anybody that America will
be cast in the role of the Cro-Magnons?

It is very easy to assume that government—ours, the
Russian, the World Court, any government—must be
right. Government represents legitimacy, tradition,
law and order, the sanction of things as they are.
These are things to be respected. And yet hear Thoreau once more. "A common and natural result of an
undue respect for law is, that you may see a file of
soldiers, colonel, captain, corporal, privates, powder-
monkeys and all, marching in admirable order over
hill and dale to the wars, against their wills, ay,
against their common sense and consciences, which
makes it very steep marching indeed."

It would be nice to hear that those against whom
we march were abandoning nuclear weapons of their
own accord, without waiting for us. But suppose they
don't? Suppose they need the example of the United
States, which our government, busy marching over
hill and dale, seems unable to give them.

If a few of us who know the peril do not step out
of that file, even if it means losing our corporal's
stripes, who will there be to head off the column from
the cliff?